THE FAMILY REUNION BIBLE

Explore – Fellowship – Give Thanks

Henry Lee Thomas

Comprehensive guide to planning a 7-day group reunion/vacation (including sample reunion charts for Orlando, Florida, and Puerto Vallarta, Mexico!)

The Family Reunion Bible

Copyright © 2021 by Henry Lee Thomas.

All rights reserved. No part of this book may be reproduced in any form or by any electronic or mechanical means, including information storage and retrieval systems, without permission in writing from the author except in the case of brief quotations included in critical articles and reviews. For information, please contact the author.

Cover Designs: Nabin Karna (Paperback), Ghanipixel (e-book, Hardcover)
Cover Photo: [Tyler Nix](...) on [Unsplash](...)
Other Photos/Illustrations: StockPhotoSecrets.com
Cartoons by: Theresa McCracken (McHumor.com)
Tables/Figures: Henry Lee Thomas

Editing: Emma Moylan

Printed and bound in the United States of America
First Edition

Names: Thomas, Henry Lee, author.
Title: The family reunion bible: explore, fellowship, give thanks / Henry Lee Thomas.
Description: Manassas, VA: Henry Thomas, 2021. | Includes bibliographical references and index.
Identifiers: LCCN 2021908643 (print) | ISBN 978-1-970144-06-2 (paperback) | ISBN 978-1-970144-07-9 (hardcover) | ISBN 978-1-970144-08-6 (ebook)
Subjects: LCSH: Family reunions. | Family reunions--Planning. | Family recreation. | Family vacations. | Families. | BISAC: TRAVEL / Special Interest / Family. | FAMILY & RELATIONSHIPS / Extended Family.
Classification: LCC GT2423.T56 2021 (print) | LCC GT2423 (ebook) | DDC 394.2--dc23.

www.FamilyReunionBible.com
hthomas@notjustformen.com

Dedication

This book is dedicated to all extended families with the hope that they realize the importance of communing together during happy times to celebrate the love of family. It is my wish that this book will be an impetus for families to get off the couch and plan their own family reunions.

Special thanks to God for giving me the vision to plan my own extended family reunions.

Family Poem

Who are we?

We are the blood, the light, the glue

We go back in time and into the future

A union that cannot be severed

Bound by our common heritage

Who dat?

We are family

By Henry Lee Thomas

Table of Contents

FOREWORD xi
INTRODUCTION 1
SECTION 1: Planning an Extended Family Reunion 5
    History 7
    Initial Planning 8
    The Team 10
        Reunion Management 10
        First Things First 11
        Roles and Responsibilities 13
        Frequency of Meeting 13
        Record Keeping 13
        Theme 14
        Décor 15
        T-Shirts 15
        Gift Baskets/Handouts 16
        Preserving the Memories 18
    Communication 20
        Email 20
        Flyers 21
        Newsletters 21
        Snail Mail 21
        Surveys 21
        Telephone 22
        Website 23
        Word of Mouth 24
        Zoom/Conference Calls 25
    The Kickoff 26
        Who, What, When and Where 26
    Budgeting 28

- **Activities** 29
- **Catering/Food** 29
- **Communications** 29
- **Conference Room/Park** 30
- **Decorations** 30
- **Gift Bag & Contents** 30
- **Keepsakes/Mementos/Souvenirs** 30
- **Lodging** 30
- **Permits and Licenses** 31
- **Printing Costs** 31
- **Prizes** 31
- **Services** 31
- **Supplies and Equipment** 32
- **Tours** 32
- **Transportation** 32
- **Miscellaneous** 32

Income and Cash Flow 33
- **Dues** 33
- **Auctions** 33
- **Bake Sales** 33
- **Cookbooks** 33
- **Miscellaneous Fundraisers** 33
- **Perform a Service** 34
- **Raffles** 34
- **Sponsors/Donations** 34
- **T-Shirt Sales** 34

Recognition 35
- **Births** 35
- **Graduations** 35
- **Marriages** 35

Retirements	35
In Memory	35
Icebreaker Awards	36
Other Accomplishments	36
Conflict Resolution	**37**
The Hatfields and the McCoys	37
In-Laws and Out-Laws	37
Reunion Code of Conduct	38
Orientation	**39**
Before You Go	39
On-Site Preparations and Set-Up	39
Registration	40
Meeting Places	40
Resort Layout	41
Location	**42**
Staycations	43
Local Area	43
Out of Area	43
Attractions	44
Beach	44
Lakefront	46
Mountain/Skiing	47
Cruise	48
Transportation	**51**
Car	51
Bus	52
Train	52
Airplane	54
Lodging	**58**
Campgrounds/Cabins	59

- **Hotels/Resorts** ... 62
- **Rental Condos** ... 62
- **Timeshares** ... 63
- **Food/Meals** ... 66
  - **All-Inclusive** ... 67
  - **Eating Out** ... 68
  - **Eating In** ... 69
  - **Catered Meals** ... 72
- **Activities** ... 73
  - **Relaxing** ... 74
  - **Indoor Activities** ... 74
  - **Let's Get Acquainted** ... 74
  - **Attractions & Festivals** ... 75
  - **Cookbooks** ... 76
  - **Escape Room** ... 77
  - **Family History** ... 77
  - **Free Time** ... 80
  - **Icebreakers** ... 80
  - **Games** ... 80
  - **Movie Night** ... 81
  - **Seminars/Workshops** ... 83
  - **Picnics** ... 84
  - **Reunion Remembrance Book** ... 84
  - **Shopping** ... 85
  - **Sunday Worship Service** ... 85
  - **Talent Show** ... 86
  - **Tours** ... 87
  - **Nightlife** ... 88
  - **Final Night Dinner/Banquet/Award Presentations** ... 88
  - **Final Morning Farewell** ... 88

Let's Rate It 89
Contingency Planning 90
Emergency Response Plan 90
COVID-19 91
Travel Insurance 92
Planning For the Next One 93
Lessons Learned 93
Gathering More Feedback 93
Putting It All Together 94
Document Publication & Distribution 94

SECTION 2: Sample Reunion Itinerary 95
Overview 97
Table A – People Locations & Game Information 99
Table B – Planned Activities 100

SECTION 3: Templates and Worksheets 103
Budget Worksheet 105
Contact List 107
Reunion Survey 108

APPENDIX A: Puerto Vallarta Newsletter 109
APPENDIX B: Reunion Code of Conduct 115
APPENDIX C: Family Reunion Checklists 119
Reunion Planning Checklist 121
Vacation Travel Checklist 123
APPENDIX D: Top Tourist Attractions in the USA 129
APPENDIX E: USA Cruise Port Locations & Destinations 133
APPENDIX F: Recommended Cruise Lines 137
APPENDIX G: Bus Transportation Options 141
Long Distance US Bus Companies 143
Mexican Bus Companies 145
Charter Bus Companies 146

APPENDIX H: Sample Costs to Rent Owner Timeshares vs From Resort	149
APPENDIX I: Popular US Festivals	153
APPENDIX J: DNA Testing Company Comparisons	157
APPENDIX K: Award Certificate Samples	161
APPENDIX L: Sample Vacation Reference Charts	173
Orlando Vacation Reference Charts	175
Puerto Vallarta Vacation Reference Charts	243
BIBLIOGRAPHY	309
ABOUT THE AUTHOR	313
INDEX	315
What Did You Think About The Family Reunion Bible?	318

FOREWORD

Long before I could afford to go on family vacations, I remember as a young boy going to the library and reading about all the wondrous places within the United States and around the world. I think I was born to travel the world. I wanted to visit all the places we discussed in school, from Africa to Europe, the gypsies in Spain, the Eiffel Tower in Paris, and so on. Maybe it was a way to remove myself from the projects where I lived with limited financial resources. Don't get me wrong, I enjoyed my childhood and we always had food on the table, we got to play, and it was a fulfilling existence, to a degree. But I wanted to do more and I decided that someday I would get to see some of those wonderful places I read and dreamed about.

My first opportunity to see other parts of the world was when I left Georgia to go to Oberlin College in Ohio. Of course there was no way I was going to go to college at home. I wouldn't be able to start experiencing the rest of the world if I did! Going to college was my first step in positioning myself to have the resources to realize my love of travel.

I also loved spending time with family though I wasn't that interested in where my relatives lived. I realized that if there was a way for me to combine my love for travel with my love for family, then that would be ideal.

The above insight led me to the idea of planning full-week vacations with extended family. I planned my first biyearly 7-day family reunion back in 2004 and have not looked back. Locations have included Orlando, Florida; Myrtle Beach, South Carolina; and Puerto Vallarta, Mexico.

Most of my family reunions have included friends and the information presented here can apply to any type of group reunion/vacation planning: family, friends, sororities, fraternities, and so on.

This book presents much of what I learned during my family reunions to assist others in planning their own family or group reunions.

You too can be a super family reunion planner!

I titled this book *The Family Reunion Bible* because traveling is a religious experience to me. That's not to say that traveling is the same as a true religion; it just is to say that when combined with family and friends, it can be a very spiritual and joyous experience that benefits the mind and soul.

Whether you are a family reunion planning novice or a guru, *The Family Reunion Bible* is your comprehensive, go-to guide for planning a successful and rewarding family reunion.

The Family Reunion Bible

INTRODUCTION

The Bible states "In the beginning God created the heavens and the earth" (Genesis n.d.). By the 6th day he created men and women and told them to be fruitful and multiply and on the 7th day they all rested and gave thanks. This was the beginning of the family.

The Cambridge Dictionary (Cambridge Dictionary n.d.) defines family as "a social group of parents, children, and sometimes grandparents, uncles, aunts, and others who are related." That's a start, but families are much more than that! This definition can be broken down into people who are part of a family based on birth, marriage, adoption, and so on. You then can talk about:

- Immediate family: spouses, parents, brothers, sisters, sons, and daughters
- Extended family: grandparents, aunts, uncles, cousins, nephews, nieces, and siblings-in-law, etc.

There are many references in the Bible that show the importance of family. In Timothy 5:8 it is stated: "Anyone who does not provide for their relatives, and especially for their own household, has denied the faith and is worse than an unbeliever" (Holy Bible n.d.).

The United Nations states that "in all parts of the world, families perform important socioeconomic and cultural functions. In spite of the many changes that have altered their roles and functions, families continue to provide the natural framework for the emotional, financial and material support essential to the growth and development of their members, particularly infants and children, and for the care of other dependents, including the elderly, disabled and infirm" (Network n.d.).

Another way to think about families is that we are all members of the "family of humans." All current Homo sapiens descended from Africa over 300,000 years ago (Human Origins n.d.). In this vein we can think of families as groups of people bound by some means: blood, friendship, common associations, and so on.

However you define it, the family serves as the backbone of society and their importance can't be overstated. It is with this understanding that this book has been written to showcase one very important activity to keep families alive: family reunions.

In the past families were more stationary and didn't move around a lot. It was very common for first, second, and third family generations to live within close proximity to each other, sometimes living in the same household. That trend began to decrease during the 1970s as people moved away for economic and other reasons. While "the multigenerational American family household is staging a comeback – driven in part by the job losses and home foreclosures of recent years but more so by demographic changes that have been gathering steam for decades" (center 2010), it's still common for family abodes to be more diverse geographically.

With all the transformations going on within families, it is more important than ever to make a conscious effort to plan good times with family. Family reunions serve this purpose. Oftentimes, families only get together for funerals. It's time we got together for a celebration of our shared connections and to build on this common bond during positive events.

Many families hold family reunions of one day or one weekend. Why not follow God's lead and have a 7-day plan instead! That's what my family has done and documented in this book.

Sometimes people dread going to family reunions because they think it might not be fun! Having to interact with relatives they don't like, relatives asking for money, awkward conversations, and so on. It doesn't have to be that way. If you think of it as a vacation and plan it that way, it's more likely that it will turn out to be a rewarding event.

Seven days allows you to take full advantage of the reason your family is vacationing together. Those first couple of days consist of getting acclimated, settled, taking care of the initial hellos. It's only by the third day that you settle into the family groove. Finally, the last couple of days allow you to enjoy the full afterglow of having extended time with your extended family and to take care of any remaining goals such as making sure you have everybody's contact information as well as enjoy those final days together!

Another important point is, with an extended family reunion, you can have private time to do things without the family at large or with smaller family groups. This allows you to get away for a bit if you are experiencing too much family time!

This book is not just for blood family members; it is also for anybody who is interested in planning their own full-week family/group reunion.

You may say I have a lot of balls calling this book *The Family Reunion Bible*. But you know what, my family and I have been having our full-week family reunions for over ten years and every time any of us talk about them to other people, we are told they don't know of any other family who does it the way we do it! I am sure the upper-crust families' do it all the time, but you don't have to be the rich and famous to partake of extended family vacations. It doesn't have to be extremely expensive. There are ways to plan it within your budget and still get the full benefit and enjoyment.

Introduction

Why I Wrote This Book

I wrote this book because there is a need. People are not taking enough time off and not connecting with friends and family as much as they should. This can result in more stress, less connectedness, and less meaning in your life. Taking 7-day vacations gives one enough time to fully benefit from taking a vacation.

The recent COVID-19 epidemic has only intensified the need to plan a long family reunion. We have been forced to stay away from family and friends for over a year because of this virus. Now is the time to recover in style by planning a long family reunion to rekindle those family relationships.

There have been many studies on the importance of taking time off. In the same way that sleep helps to clear the brain of clutter and to repair itself (Shaffer 2016), going on vacation and/or taking time off helps to declutter and heal the conscious mind and emotional well-being (Hollinger 2017).

> 🖐 The average person needs 7 days of sleep per night and 7 days per vacation!

People are leaving vacation days on the table! Particularly those of us in the United States. The US has one of the lowest average number of vacation days in the world, yet Americans still don't take all the vacation days they are entitled to. The average American gets 15 days of vacation while most of the world gets between 20 and 30 days (Wikipedia n.d.). The Expedia Group found that in 2018, "American vacation deprivation levels are at a five-year high" (group 2018).

There are even references in the Bible that imply people should take vacations. In Mark, Jesus tells his apostles to "Come away by yourselves to a desolate place and rest a while" (Bible, New International Version 2011).

The importance of family should not be disputed, but we tend to forget that. It is time for us to resurrect our communion with family, and what better way to do it than participating in a family reunion. Now that the end of the COVID-19 pandemic is in our sight, let us declare a new epiphany:

The Season of Family Reunions

The Family Reunion Bible

The end of COVID-19 should be a wake-up call for all of us on the importance of getting together with family. Now is the time to jumpstart your family reunions, and this book will help you to get out of the blocks.

How to Use This Book

This book can be used in the following ways:

1. Start with the first section and move sequentially to the end.
2. Read just the sections you need help with in planning your reunion.
3. As a reference during a family reunion for ideas on things to do.

You may find that you will take advantage of each of the above uses during the course of planning and enjoying your vacations.

So let's get ready, set, and going on planning and enjoying many memorable extended family and friend reunions in the future!

SECTION 1: Planning an Extended Family Reunion

👉 Section Highlights

- History
- Communication
- Income & Cash Flow
- Orientation
- Lodging
- Contingency Planning

- Initial Planning
- The Kickoff
- Recognition
- Location
- Food/Meals
- Planning For the Next One

- The Team
- Budgeting
- Conflict Resolution
- Transportation
- Activities

The Family Reunion Bible

History

> **And let us consider how to stir up one another to love and good works, not neglecting to meet together, as is the habit of some, but encouraging one another, and all the more as you see the Day drawing near** (Bible, New International Version 2011, Hebrews 10:24-25).

It is impossible to know when the first family reunion was held as that event is unlikely to have been documented. We do find references to family reunions in the Bible between Joseph and Jacob, his father and everyone in their houses.

Joseph sends his brothers to bring their father, Jacob, to Egypt (Bible, New International Version 2011, Genesis 45:9–13). Jacob gathers all the family (Bible, New International Version 2011, Genesis 46:5–25, 26) and heads to Egypt. Joseph gathers the four people in his family, including himself, to meet them, and the number of people participating in this family reunion numbered seventy (Bible, New International Version 2011, Genesis 46:27). When Joseph and Jacob (Israel) see each other again, they embrace and weep in a joy-filled family reunion (Bible, New International Version 2011, Genesis 46:29).

African American family reunions "date back to Emancipation, as a way for former slaves to reconnect with their family members from whom they had been separated and also in response to the great migration of more than six million African Americans from the rural south to urban, industrial cities in the north, Midwest, and west, between 1916 and 1970 (Sula Hood n.d.)." This tradition has carried on has become an important celebration in the African American diaspora. As a result of genealogy DNA testing, some descendants of slaves and slave owners are now having joint family reunions to come to terms with their common heritage and to join together as one.

The US Congress designated the period between Mother's Day, May 13, 1984, and Father's Day, June 17, 1984, as Family Reunion Month (99th Congress, 1st Session 1985) but July is known as National Family Reunion Month (Wikipedia, The Free Encyclopedia 2020). These proclamations make it official and give you permission to starting planning your own family reunions!

No matter what your ethnic or racial background is, if you have family you will benefit from having a family reunion. Even if you are a member of a group that considers themselves to be family, family reunions may be for you.

Family reunions have been an important part of our history. Maybe it's time for you to jump on the bandwagon!

Initial Planning

> **The plans of the diligent lead to profit as surely as haste leads to poverty** (Bible, New International Version 2011, Proverbs 21:5)

One of the big differences between having an afternoon group barbeque in the backyard and having a 7-day group reunion in an offsite location is forward planning. You can plan your barbeque on the spur of the moment days before the event, but you are destined to fail unless you plan your 7-day reunion well in advance.

You should plan your 7-day family reunion a year or more in advance of the event if possible. It can be done quicker but the more time you have the better.

> **When planning an extended group reunion, remember that people will response on "island time" and not "business time"!**

All family reunions start with an idea. Someone has to decide they want to have a family reunion, and that person or persons have to plant the seed with other potential attendees.

When planning a family reunion, it is good to start with the *end in mind*. Close your eyes and think about the experience you and your family want to have. Imagine how you are feeling, what you are smelling, and the activities that are bringing your family the most joy. This exercise will help to get you in the right mood for planning your great family event.

Next, an assessment has to be made to determine the degree of interest in putting on this show. This interest can be determined in the following ways:

- Make calls to select people you feel are most likely to be interested.
- Send out email blasts to all family members.
- Generate a simple survey and send out a mass distribution to every single person who you feel has any probability of being interested.
- Post a notice in any group affiliated document.

The intent of this first communication is not to provide a whole lot of detail at this point; it's just to determine general interest so an assessment can be made as to the validity of the idea.

Section 1

Once it is determined that there is interest, the person(s) who thought of the idea need to pull together an interim team to start the preliminary planning.

The Team

> **Two are better than one, because they have a good return for their labor: If either of them falls down, one can help the other up. But pity anyone who falls and has no one to help them up.** (Bible, New International Version 2011, Ecclesiastes 4: 9-10)

You will want to pull together a few people who are very interested in helping to plan the event. It doesn't necessarily take a lot of people and you don't want too many at first, as this could hurt your effort to get the planning off the ground. It's more important to have the right type of people: those who can get along, maybe have some experience in some element of the planning, are committed to the process, and so on.

I was basically the only person on the planning committee for my first couple of reunions, but I already had many years of planning my own immediate family vacations. I soon realized though that getting other people involved would make the process a little bit easier. Still, my team ended up being about three people, including me.

You will need to decide the number of people it makes sense to have on your team. The less experience you have, the more people you need to have on the team. But remember, *too many cooks spoil the stew!*

Reunion Management
If you want to increase the odds of having a successful family reunion, you need to *organize for success*. This means managing the planning of your reunion like a project team. A project, in general, is an activity that has a distinct beginning and end with a defined scope and that usually requires resources. Your project is to plan your family reunion in a finite amount of time so that everything is done and on time and within budget to have a successful reunion. You accomplish this goal by enlisting your planning team to manage the successful execution of your next great family reunion!

There are five steps to project management (Project Management Institute 2017):

- Initiating: Deciding whether you will do this, identifying goals, etc.
- Planning: Selecting the team, creating the budget and schedule, etc.
- Executing: Carrying out the tasks identified in the planning stage.

- Controlling and Monitoring: Tracking your progress and tweaking things as necessary to keep on schedule to finish the project on time and within budget.
- Closing: For family reunions, things don't stop with the beginning of the reunion; you are just getting started! You still have a reunion to run. When the reunion is over, then you can begin your shutdown.

To ensure that all team members are on the same page, it is beneficial to create mission and vision statements. Your family reunion planning mission statement would be a short statement of the purpose of the reunion, what the overall goal is and how you plan to achieve it. Your vision statement would go into a little more detail on your mission.

For example, if you are planning a family history reunion, sample mission and vision statements are as follows:

- Our family reunion mission is to pull together all generations of our family and to celebrate family members from the past, present and to set the foundation for future family members. We will accomplish this by celebrating our faith in God, our values, health, work ethic, and love for family.
- Our family reunion vision is to include a wide swath of our relatives, to locate and include long-lost relatives, to provide knowledge and information about our ancestors, and to strengthen our family unit to sustain all challenges and to provide heritage information for our young people.

Finally, to make sure you have an optimally performing team, you will want to define clear roles and responsibilities so you all don't step all over each other.

First Things First
The most critical first decisions you will need to make are the time and location of your family reunion. This is crucial because lodging and transportation may need to be reserved up to a year in advance.

If you are going to a popular location with limited lodging availability, the most desirable options may already be taken up to a year in advance. It's all about supply and demand. You want to know as soon as possible what your location and dates are so you can at least monitor availability on an ongoing basis, so you know when the critical time is to make a commitment.

If you will be flying to your destination, the major airlines begin to list their flights around eleven months in advance. You need to know where you are going at that point so you can start monitoring prices and see when the prices drop to your price point.

You don't want to get into a situation where you select a date and find out that family members have already planned something for that date. To avoid this problem, you want to set a date for your family reunion at least a year in advance if possible.

Most people schedule family reunions in the summer when children are out of school, and that is when all of mine have been scheduled. Because of this, summer family reunions can be more expensive since everybody has the same idea and is competing for the same lodging options.

Another popular time for family reunions is spring break though if family members live in different parts of the country their spring break may not land on the same week.

It would be difficult to gain consensus on the time to have a family reunion, so I would recommend limited discussions with family members on dates and then having the planning team select a date and communicate it to the family. Again, if this is done well ahead of schedule, it gives everyone time to fit it into their schedule.

Selecting a location for the reunion takes a little more care and is discussed in a later section of this book.

Another important factor to consider is the size of your reunion. The more people involved, the more planning is required. You need to consider whether you will be planning a small, medium, or large reunion:

- Small (less than 20 people)
- Medium (between 20 and 50 people)
- Large (greater than 50 people)

Planning a reunion for 10 people is a lot different than planning for 100 people. The size impacts what type of accommodations will work for you, what types of activities are feasible, what the common expenses are likely to be, and so on.

Of course to answer the size question, you need to know how many people are interested in participating, so answering this question is the first step to answering the reunion size question.

For some additional information on group travel and some family reunion statistics, check out goruptravel.org (grouptravel.org n.d.).

Roles and Responsibilities

Once you have selected your team, roles and responsibilities have to be assigned. You will be deciding who will be doing what? If the team or reunion is big enough, you may want to create committees to be responsible for certain aspects of the reunion.

At a minimum you will have a family reunion chairperson who is responsible for the overall planning and success of the reunion. Other roles will be assigned as needed and may include:

- Treasurer
- Photographer
- Decorations
- Fundraising
- Entertainment
- Tracking down family members

Team members may have multiple roles and may change roles during the course of the planning.

Frequency of Meeting

The team should meet weekly during the first month or two of planning. During this time you want to:

- Assign roles and responsibilities
- Generate contact list for family members (see section 3 for sample list)
- Close on the location and dates for the reunion
- Determine the theme of the reunion
- Create a budget
- Provide preliminary reunion information to family members

After the first couple of months, the team can probably meet once or twice a month and ad hoc as necessary. The key is to keep the planning going and making sure tasks and assignments are being completed.

Record Keeping

It is important to keep good records on the family reunion. Key records to keep include:

- Family member contact lists
    - Complete list of all family members to be contacted
    - Many may not attend the reunion

- Lodging payments
    - If payments are not being made directly to the facility
    - Total lodging cost, payments, balance
- Products purchased
    - Supplies, decorations, etc.
- Services paid for
    - Catering, cleaning, etc.
- Attendance list
    - These are the people who will actually be attending the event
    - Name (primary contact name and name of other immediate family members), telephone number, email address
- Reservations made
    - Meals, shuttle services, tours, etc.

There are a number of ways to get the above records: paper, hardcopy books, computer spreadsheets, record keeping software, and so on.

Either the reunion organizer, bookkeeper, or treasurer should be assigned to keep the above records. The planning team members should review the above records during all meetings.

Theme
You don't necessarily need to have a theme for your family reunion, but it is a big plus as it can provide more focus for your event and allows you to plan around that central theme. For example, for my family reunion in Puerto Vallarta, Mexico, our theme was "Fiesta Time" to match the location and we planned activities to match that theme. We have had a different theme for each of our family reunions.

Your theme can be anything you like or could be associated with something relevant to your family. Example themes include:

- Anniversaries, birthdays, and other family special events
- Disney/theme parks
- Education
- Ethnic (African American, Greek, Italian, Native American, etc.)
- Family history/genealogy
- Family talent (talent shows, etc.)
- Food
- Hawaiian
- Patriotic

- Related to the reunion location
- Seasonal (spring, summer, etc.)
- Sports/Olympics
- Wild West

Once you have selected your theme, you want to weave that theme into your activities, foods, newsletters, and so on. The theme sets the stage for the rest of your reunion planning.

Décor

Once you have determined your theme, you can get to work on planning the décor for your reunion. Your décor will be primarily set up in the primary indoor meeting place for your reunion. That could be the lodging of one of the participants, a conference room, and so on. It will include decorations, displays, items for sale, reference material and so on.

You can keep the same decorations throughout the reunion or change them day to day to reflect the day's activities. You want to have fun with it but make sure you manage your budget and don't go too far with your décor.

Take advantage of items owned by family members who may have items that match your theme. You will want to identify these items as soon as possible so you will have good insight into what things did to be purchased.

Also, take advantage of any artistic ability participants may have, such as painting, building things, designing, and so on.

Overall you want your décor to complement your theme to help set the mood for your reunion.

T-Shirts

T-shirts can show off your family symbol. If you want to show your swag, unity, or colors, then matching T-shirts is the way to go. Your group will look more professional if you step out in your family uniform!

T-shirts can also be a big part of your family reunion décor as well as your defining your group (they also help to keep track of everyone when the group is out and about. Just look for those T-shirts!).

For family reunions, you would normally have the following on the front of the T-shirts:

- Family name
- Family crest or a symbol/picture representing some aspect of the family/theme
- Location of the event
- Date.

The back of the shirts can be blank or have any additional information you want to include.

You can be creative though and design your T-shirts any way you want.

There are numerous online websites you can use to order your T-shirts or you may have access to local businesses that can produce them. You would primarily wear your T-shirts during group activities when you would be around other people.

You will want to assign one person who would be responsible for getting the T-shirts designed, purchased, and distributed. Factors to be considered include:

- Overall design
- Color(s)
- Sizes
- Quantities
- Quality
- Cost
- Collecting payments
- Distribution (before or at the event)

Don't wait until the last minute to order your T-shirts as you don't want to risk not having them on time or having to pay extra to expedite their delivery.

Gift Baskets/Handouts

Another important decision to make is whether to have gift baskets or handouts for all participants of the reunion. At a minimum you will want to consider providing the following items to everyone:

- Attendee list
- Detailed list of planned activities
- Everyone's cell phone number
- Everyone's lodging location/room numbers
- Folder for papers
- House rules
- Itinerary/schedule of events
- Maps and brochures

- Name tags (if everyone is not known by everyone)
- Regional gifts reflecting your reunion theme or location

You may also want to provide gift bags for attendees. This would be a nice touch to include depending on your budget. These gifts would be keepsakes or items that participants can use. Remember to stay within your budget when planning what will go in your gift bags.

> ✋ **The 2020 Oscar's committee provided gift bags worth more than $200,000 for its biggest nominees. We aren't talking about anything like that for your reunion gift bags!**

You don't have to spend a lot of money to put together a nice gift bag. Some items you can include are:

- Candies or other sweets
- Candles
- Cookbooks (you may want to sell these instead)
- Key chains
- Koozies (for keeping drinks colder on hot days)
- Lip balm
- Lottery tickets available for the reunion location
- Luggage tags
- Magnets
- Mini flashlight
- Mini photo albums
- Noisemakers
- Notebooks
- Paper hand fan (for hot days)
- Personalized pencils
- Personalized pens
- Sunglass straps
- Water bottles

Don't forget the actual bags you will put your items in! Some of the considerations for the bags are:

- Size (make sure it can accommodate all the items needing to go in it)
- Rigidity/thickness

- Color
- Exterior image (standard or customized)

Don't select your gift bags until you have closed on with will go in the bags!

Preserving the Memories

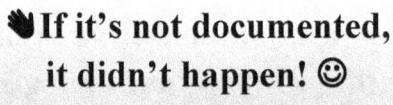

All kidding aside, you won't regret documenting your family vacations so you can relive the joy in the form of pictures, videos, and so on.

It is important to document your family vacation so you have more than your memory to fall back on to reminisce on the fun you had and all the reconnections you made during your family vacation.

What's the point of having a family vacation if you don't have anything to help you remember it?

So how do you document your family reunion? You would have already started if you provided handouts and/or gift bags to attendees. These are tangible items that will help jog the memory of participants when they hold and view the item. Many people will keep these items in a special place so they can be retrieved when they want to relive the event.

They say pictures are worth a thousand words and they are correct. Having pictures of your family reunion provides a visual remembrance of all the events and people participating in your grand event. These pictures can include both still pictures and movies/videos.

You can have one person responsible for taking both still pictures and videos or you can have separate individuals for each of these activities.

Even if you have a dedicated photographer/videographer, you will find that other family members will also be performing these activities on their own. It is important that the other family members provide their pictures/videos to the person dedicated to these activities so all pictures/videos will be available to be put into a final product.

The final picture/video product would be available to all participants soon after the reunion.

It can be overly expensive to provide printed pictures to attendees. The gold standard these days is to provide each attendee with a USB drive or CD with all the pictures/videos on them. These devices are very inexpensive and can hold a lot of data. Attendees can then selectively print out the pictures they are most interested in to be framed or used in some other way, and the videos can be played directly from the USB drive or loaded onto a computer to play from there.

You may want to provide a good group picture or collage of pictures to attendees though so they have one ready-made visual keepsake.

Communication

> **Do not let any unwholesome talk come out of your mouths, but only what is helpful for building others up according to their needs, that it may benefit those who listen.** (Bible, New International Version 2011, Ephesians 4:29)

In order to communicate with family members about the reunion, you need to know where they are! You probably already know where many of your relatives are, though you may not have contact information for them, and you may not have a clue as to the location of some of your other relatives. Therefore, one of your first tasks is to locate your relatives and to have a means to contact them. There are a number of ways to find your relatives, including the following:

- Start with the ones you have contact information for and ask them for contact information on the relatives you need contact information for.
- Utilizing directories for organizations your relative belongs to.
- Hiring a professional investigator.

Once the team has been selected and has a way to contact your relatives, it is important to determine when and how to communicate information about the family vacation to potential and actual participants. You will use multiple communication methods throughout the planning based on the specific need, what needs to be communicated and who needs to be contacted.

Email
You will want to get the email address of as many family members as possible. Email is one of the most efficient methods of communicating. It's fast and generally doesn't cost anything to send.

Most people at least have access to email via their cell phones even if they don't have a computer. For those family members who don't have access to email, they can be contacted by other means.

You want to make sure you have as complete an email list as possible and keep track of those potential attendees who don't have an email address so you can make sure you get the information out to the non-email users soon after sending emails to the email users.

Flyers

Flyers would usually be one-page documents that provide high-level information on the upcoming reunion. These flyers would be handed out directly or mailed to the recipient.

Newsletters

Once one document exceeds one page, you generally would be moving from a flyer to a newsletter. The newsletter provides more detail than can be communicated on a flyer. Your first newsletter would provide key details on the family reunion, including date, location, theme, and some of the other significant information. Additional newsletters would follow as necessary. You should plan on sending two to four newsletters during the course of the planning.

Your newsletters would primarily be sent via email, but you may need to distribute some manually or via snail mail. If you have a bunch of family members living in the same area, you could send a package of newsletters to one responsible person in the area who would then distribute them to family members in their local area.

You can use Microsoft Word, Microsoft Publisher, or other software to generate your newsletters. I use Publisher for mine. A sample of one of my newsletters is provided in appendix A for reference.

Snail Mail

Communicating information via the US Postal Service is more expensive than the other methods as you have the cost of envelopes and postage. It also takes a longer period of time for the recipient to receive the information. It may be quicker than the old pony express or stagecoach method, but it takes days compared to the almost instantaneous delivery of email.

You should use snail mail (USPS, FedEx, UPS, etc.) sparingly for text information and use it primarily for shipping products as required.

Surveys

You may want to use surveys to help make key reunion-related decisions, such as the location of the family reunion. Some of the reunion items you may want to solicit feedback on via a survey are:

- Location

- Activities/games
- Dates
- Theme
- Type (condos, cruise, camping, etc.)

You will want to limit the number of options people have to choose from in your survey. I would recommend you have some informal conversations with family members to get a general feel for their preferences and then get with the planning team to decide on what the options will be. You would send the survey out with the options determined by the planning team.

You can either send hardcopy copies of the survey via email, snail mail, and so on. or you can utilize one of the survey websites. Some of the survey websites allow you to generate a limited size and number of surveys without cost. In most cases you only need to utilize the free options available on one of these websites and not have to use any of the paid options. Some of the available survey websites to consider are:

- Free Online Surveys – https://freeonlinesurveys.com/
- Crowd Signal – https://crowdsignal.com/
- Survey Monkey – https://www.surveymonkey.com/
- Survey Legend – https://www.surveylegend.com/
- Survey Planet – https://surveyplanet.com/
- Type Form – https://www.typeform.com/

You will need to go to the website of the survey you want to use, create an account, and follow the directions to set up and execute your survey. Your family members would need to go to the website to fill out the survey online after you provide them with a link to the survey.

If you are mathematically inclined, you can also create your own survey using Microsoft Excel.

A sample reunion survey is provided in section 3 (Templates and Worksheets).

Telephone
For quick conversations, the telephone is your friend. You will pick up the phone when you need answers to questions right away or when you need to pass on information to someone and you want to make sure they get the message as opposed to waiting for them to respond to an email, for example. This is why it is important for you to have a comprehensive and complete contact list.

If the person has both landline and cell phones, make sure you have both numbers.

You will especially find that having everyone's cell phone number will be immensely beneficial during the family reunion.

Website

If you happen to have a family website, you will find it very useful as a go-to spot for family members to go-to get up-to-date information on your family reunion. That way they don't have to wait for a newsletter or email (which would only provide limited information).

I generate a separate family reunion section on my family website for upcoming family reunions. That section provides one with just about everything one would want to know about the upcoming event and they can refer back to that information at any time day or night.

Having this central real-time information hub is a common source where family members can always find information without having to track down someone to ask a question about the event.

If you don't have a family website, you may want to consider creating one. Besides for family reunions, this site can provide other useful information to family members and keep them updated on all the shenanigans and important information going on in the family.

If you are going to create a family website/blog, the first thing you need to do is decide on a domain name. The domain name basically provides the "address" for your website so that your web browser knows where to go to find your website. The format of the domain name is:

> www.DomainName.com
>
> "DomainName" is the name you want to give your website and "com" is the domain name extension.

For example, if your family name is "Brown" and you want to use your family name for your domain, you can select BrownFamily.com, BrownFamilyBlog.com, and so on.

Your domain name can be anything you want it to be as long as that name is not owned by anyone else. Note that you can't have any spaces between the letters in your domain name.

In addition, .com is not the only extension available to you for your domain name (though .com is the most popular one). Some of the available domain name extensions are:

- .com
- .org
- .net
- .edu (limited to specific higher educational institutions)
- .gov (limited to United States government entities)
- .mil (limited to divisions, services and agencies of the United States Department of Defense

There are many more domain name extensions though.

You can purchase your domain name from many sources, including the following:

- Flippa
- HostGator
- Hostwinds
- GoDaddy
- NameCheap
- NotJustForMen (Lower cost GoDaddy reseller)
- SnapNames

There are many more places you can purchase your domain name also.

In addition, you will need to find a place to host your website. You don't have to host your website with the same company you purchased your domain name from but you can. Where you host your website is more important than where you purchase your domain name. You want to host your website with a company with good customer service and who is reliable with all the services you need to run your site.

If you don't have experience developing a website, many of the hosting companies have easy-to-use web hosting software you can use or you could hire someone to develop and manage your site as a last resort.

Word of Mouth
Have you ever played the game where you line up a bunch of people, whisper in the ear of the person on one end who whispers what you told them to the person next to them and repeat this game until the whisper gets to the person at the other end of the line?

Chances are the message that the last person received is somewhat different than the initial message. That's the problem with word-of-mouth information. Something tends to get lost in the translation. Because of this, you will want to minimize the amount of information that is communicated only via word of mouth. If you do communicate something by word of mouth, it's a good idea to follow up with another form of communication (email, etc.) to make sure the information got through accurately. The other option is to ask the other person to repeat what they thought they heard from you to verify that is what you actually said.

Zoom/Conference Calls
Zoom is the newest kid on the block as far as communication methods are concerned. It allows for the masses to participate in conference calls and is a good option for family reunion planning meetings and briefings to family members on the event. I use Zoom for my family reunion planning and briefings.

Currently, the following pricing plans are available with Zoom:

- Free
    - Host up to 100 participants
    - Group meetings for up to 40 minutes
    - Unlimited one-on-one meetings
- $149.90 per year per license
    - Host up to 100 participants
    - Group meeting for up to 30 hours
    - Social media streaming
    - 1 GB cloud recording per license

There are additional plans for businesses, but you wouldn't need any of those plans for your purpose.

There are other video calling apps with free options other than Zoom that may work for you. Some others to consider are:

- Skype Meet Now
- Cisco Webex
- Google Meet
- Microsoft Teams
- Starleaf
- Jitsi Meet
- Whereby

The Kickoff

Traveling, in general, can be a religious experience if done right. If you add family to the mix, it can be darn right holy! That's why it is important to get it right and to make time for it.

Once your family reunion planning team has completed all its preliminary activities, it is time to have a kickoff meeting. The kickoff meeting is a meeting to communicate the key information about the reunion to all who are interested in participating. It's good to have a meeting so people have the opportunity to ask questions, but you can also kick off things by sending an email or newsletter.

Whether you have an actual meeting or send out the information via email or newsletter, the following spells out the information you want to communicate:

Who, What, When and Where
- Who: Who is this information for (parents and siblings, all family members, members in a particular geographical area, etc.)? You want to be clear on the scope of people you are trying to include. If friends or others can be included, make that clear. My family reunions always include friends of some family members. The more, the merrier!
- What: Be clear that this is a family reunion and the scope of the reunion (7 days long, a long weekend, theme, purpose, etc.)
- When: Provide them with the date(s) of the reunion. Give the specific dates. If you haven't decided on the exact dates, provide the time frame (spring, summer, etc.) If you are looking for feedback on the dates, provide a due date in which the feedback is needed and let them know you will be selecting the dates based on the feedback you have received by that due date.
- Where: Where is this baby going to take place! You really should have the location nailed down prior to the kickoff meetings. Any surveys or feedback should occur prior to the kickoff meeting. If too many of the key details are still fuzzy at this point, people won't have enough clarity to determine if it's something they can or want to participant in.

During this meeting you want to convey to people that *"this is want we are going to do."* They need to feel that you know what you are doing. At the same time, you want to get them excited at the prospect of participating in this event and give them all the information they need to plan around it.

You will also want to provide people with an estimate of what the overall cost will be to attend the family reunion. This includes their direct payments as well as their portion of the common expenses.

In addition, you will also want to communicate where people can go to get additional information about the event. That could be a contact person on the planning team, the family website, and so on.

Questions to Ask

Once you have completed your presentation (if you decide to have a meeting), you will want to open things up to questions. If there are any questions you can't answer, make a note of them and provide answers later. You may also want to come up with a frequently asked questions (FAQs) list to answer a few questions you think people may have. An FAQ is especially beneficial if you end up not having a meeting but send a kickoff email/newsletter instead.

It is also beneficial to send out minutes after the kickoff meetings. The minutes would summarize everything that was discussed at the meeting, along with answers to all the questions asked.

Budgeting

> **After all the money had been spent throughout Egypt and Canaan, all the Egyptians came to Joseph and demanded, "Give us food! Why should we die right in front of you? Our money is spent!"** (Bible, New International Version 2011, Genesis 47:15)

Budget: "A budget is an estimation of revenue and expenses over a specified future period of time and is usually compiled and reevaluated on a periodic basis. Budgets can be made for a person, a group of people, a business, a government, or just about anything else that makes and spends money" (Ganti 2020).

The more people participating in your family reunion, the more important a budget becomes. You need to have a good idea of what your expenses will be and where the income will be coming from.

As part of the planning committee, you will be responsible for documenting the expected expenses and identifying where the funds will come from to pay those expenses. You even need to track the status of payments family members make directly outside the planning team so you can snug those family members that they have a payment coming due.

I sometimes secure accommodations for family members and have them pay me in full or I may set up a payment plan so they can pay me in installments. I need to keep very good records when I accept installment payments so there is no issue with what has been paid or what the balance is.

> If you don't have a lot of confidence that you will receive payments from a family member, don't accept installment payments from them!

In general, you will want family members to pay for their lodging and individual transportation costs directly, so the only thing the planning team needs to track is when those payments are paid so we can check them off.

The planning team will primarily budget for all the common expenses, but your budget should also provide everyone with an estimate of what their overall family reunion cost will be.

Microsoft Excel or another spreadsheet is your friend for keeping track of your budget. You can also use it for creating some of the other templates (game scorecard, etc.) you may need for your reunion. A sample budget worksheet is provided in section 3 (Templates and Worksheets).

Some of the possible items the planning team may need to budget for are the following:

Activities
Accounting for all your activities is difficult to do but if you chose to, document your major activities and estimate their cost. Make sure you include your free activities in this list as sometimes activities thought to be free may turn out to have a cost. Including these free activities also helps when mapping out your reunion schedule.

When you document your activities, make a note on if you need to make reservations for any of your activities or if they require a refundable fee to hold the reservation.

Catering/Food
Many families decide to have their food catered for some of their major functions, such as a dance party or for formal presentations. The cost to cater may not only include the food. Make sure you capture all the costs, including the facility, servers, equipment rentals, and so on.

Communications
If you are just sending making non-toll telephone calls, emails and maybe faxes, you may not have any communication costs but more than likely you will. Possible communication costs include:

- Envelopes
- Information packets
- Invitations
- Newsletters
- Postage
- Website fees

Conference Room/Park

You may need a conference room or a park if you plan on having a function that requires a lot of space or if you need special equipment that these facilities provide, which could include food catering if you don't want to handle that yourself. Similar to catering above, make sure you capture all the costs, including the food, servers, equipment rentals, and so on.

Decorations

It is important to decide on your theme early on as this may impact the type and cost of decorations for your reunion. You can go as big or as little as you want when it comes to decorations, so the costs can vary a lot. You may be able to reduce the cost by utilizing items already owned by family members.

Select decorations that enhance or complements your theme. For example, if your reunion will be held in Mexico and your theme is "A Mexican Fiesta," select fiesta-related decorations such as fiesta-themed banners, paper products, maracas, and so on. Don't forget about your clothes as you may want to decorate yourselves as well!

Gift Bag & Contents

If you will be giving out gift bags, don't forget about the bag itself when deciding what you want to put in the bag. Gift bags can have a significant cost depending on what items you decide to include, so tread carefully if you have a tight budget or if it is a challenge collecting reunion fees from family members.

Keepsakes/Mementos/Souvenirs

The above comments on gift bag contents apply to keepsakes, mementos, and souvenirs as well. You may include some of these items in your gift bags but others may be for purchase by family members. I have found that family members who didn't even participate in the reunion still wanted some of our mementos, so don't forget to query all family members to determine interest, not just those attending the reunion.

Lodging

It's hard to forget about lodging costs but it's easy to underestimate them. The estimates you get a year ahead of your reunion may be significantly more one month before the start of your reunion. The sooner you nail down your lodging costs the better. Nailed down means that you have fully paid for your lodging or at least paid a deposit to guarantee the cost.

If family members will be securing their own lodging directly, make sure you make them aware of the potential cost of dallying.

Permits and Licenses

It is easy to forget about the costs of permits and licenses, especially for things that may be free in some states/counties and require a fee in others. You must have identified what activities you will be participating in before you can determine what permits and license fees you must budget for. For example, if you will be going fishing, will you need a fishing license? If you will be going to a state park, will you need to pay for a permit?

Some facilities have limited sites. If you will need such a site reserve it well in advance or risk the facility being sold out. For example, if you will need to reserved, a covered picnic pavilion there will be a limited number of these, and once they are gone, they are gone.

Printing Costs
- Ink
- Invitations
- Family tree chart
- Newsletter
- Paper.

Prizes

If you will be having games or contests as part of your reunion, you will need to provide prizes to the winners! These prizes can be a simple and inexpensive as a certificate you print out on your computer to a trophy to something more expensive. The sky's the limit! Make sure that your account for these costs in your budget.

Services

If you don't have a family member who will donate their time to be your reunion photographer/videographer, you will need to hire out for this service. Make sure you understand exactly what is included in this service (CDs, memory books, frames, prints, etc.) and the pricing method (minimum price, hourly, etc.).

Maybe you want to farm out the full planning to an expert for your family reunion (don't do that though, as you won't need this book then!). This would be a last option though, and I know you have the skill to pull yours off yourself or with your team!

Other potential services to consider include:

- Catering
- Cleanup
- Clowns
- DJs

Supplies and Equipment
Supplies can be anything from paper and pencils to boxes, tape, and so on. Equipment can be staplers, screwdrivers, hole-punch, and so forth. These are usually low-cost items, but you do need to give them some thought as the list could be much bigger than you initially thought.

Tours
Group tours can be a fun family reunion activity. They allow you to get together as a group and let somebody else take care of the details. You may be able to negotiate a group discount for your reunion depending on the size of your group.

Transportation
Group transportation costs may include the cost of a bus if you will be busing family members to the reunion or a shuttle service for transporting members to different activities.

Miscellaneous
There will always be unique expenses realized in all family reunions or common expenses that are often overlooked. Try to capture these.

Income and Cash Flow

Dues

The purpose of the dues collected from family members is to pay for all the common expenses associated with the family reunion.

It takes money to pull off an extended family vacation and sometimes more money is needed than the participants can directly contribute. In these cases fundraisers come to the rescue! Once you collect dues, you may find that your income cupboard is still a little bare.

There are many ways to raise money to supplement the income available from your family vacationers. Below are some of the options:

Auctions

If family members have items of value that they are willing to give away, why not have an auction? People love auctions as they think they are getting something for less than its true value. You may want to give it a try.

Bake Sales

I know you have cooks in the house, right? What family doesn't have good cooks? Put that skill to work by having a bake sale.

Cookbooks

After you have finished your bake sale, write down all those recipes and publish a cookbook. You can sell this cookbook not just to family members but to anybody who loves to cook and is looking for some new recipes to try out.

Miscellaneous Fundraisers
- Lottery tickets
- Personalized calendars

Perform a Service
If you really want to get down and dirty, you can perform a service to raise money. Think of car washes, lawn work, garage sales, and so on.

Raffles
Raffles are another good way to raise money. You can sell raffle tickets for televisions, cameras, trips, and so on. People pay, say, one dollar at a chance to win an item that costs significantly more. You raise more money than the cost of the item you are giving away and the profit is yours.

Sponsors/Donations
Family reunions usually don't include sponsorships but if your event includes raising money for a special cause or if you need an extra infusing of cash, sponsorships may be in your future. Some ideas for a sponsorship follows:

- Sell ads on your family website or reunion book (see, I told you these would come in handy!). Try to identify businesses that can benefit from your reunion location theme, clothes, etc. For example, if you will be wearing family reunion T-shirts, see if the company that made your shirts are interested in advertising with you. Extra credit if you advertised the business on your T-shirts!
- If you will be renting or purchasing any type of equipment for you reunion, maybe you can have signs advertising those businesses for a fee. People would be able to see that equipment in use and may want to know more about where you purchased it from.
- If any family members have a business and want to advertise that business, maybe they would be willing to donate some money to your reunion for some advertising.

T-Shirt Sales
If you will be purchasing T-shirts for your reunion, you can tack on a couple of extra dollars to the cost and use the extra toward your other reunion costs. You can also sell reunion T-shirts to family members who are not attending the reunion but would like a T-shirt anyway.

Recognition

> **Do not withhold good from those to whom it is due, when it is in your power to act.** (Bible, New International Version 2011, Proverbs 3:27)

I always like to recognize accomplishments and key milestones of family members during my family reunions. Generally, you would include milestones occurring during the last year or since the last reunion.

Below are some examples of things to acknowledge:

Births
Capture all births up to the month prior to the reunion as it may be difficult to add at the last minute if you have printouts with the information.

Graduations
Include all kinds of graduations. School graduations should start at least with elementary school (and maybe preschool). Go crazy with it and try not to leave anybody out.

Marriages
If the married couple is at the reunion, you may also want to include some additional recognition for them during the reunion.

Retirements
This is a big one. Include how many years they have worked and ask them what they plan on doing during their new phase of life.

In Memory
Celebrate the life of those who have passed. This can be a tricky one. Think about who will be attending to help you decide how to address this topic.

Icebreaker Awards

This is a fun category. Think of things that will make people laugh or something that surprises people (nothing that will hurt anyone's feelings though). I actually provide certificates to the prize winners!

Some examples of categories I have used are:

- First person to pay their dues
- First person to pay their lodging fees
- Person with the most children present
- Person with the most grandchildren present
- Person with the longest name
- Person with the most tattoos
- Person who has lived in the most places
- Person with the most degrees

Other Accomplishments

Any other accomplishments you can think of should be on the table. There may be something unique to your family or geographic area.

Whatever family accomplishments you want to celebrate, a family reunion is a good time to do it while many family members are together to share in the moment.

Conflict Resolution

> **A gentle response diverts anger, but a harsh statement incites fury.** (Bible, New International Version 2011, Proverbs 15:1)

The Hatfields and the McCoys
You may be familiar with the Hatfield and McCoy feud. It was a decade-long feud between two families living "along the Tug Fork of the Big Sandy River which snaked along the boundary between Kentucky and West Virginia (Wikipedia, the free encyclopedia 2021)."

Maybe you have some relatives who don't get along. How do you handle that at a family reunion?

- Attendance list: One thing you can do to minimize the chance of conflict is to carefully select the people who will be attending the event to the degree possible. This may sound counterintuitive to some of the initial recommendations for "casting a wide net" when looking for reunion participants but the devil is in the details. You first cast a wide net and then you see what you have caught. If you have caught aggressive fish or those who don't play well with others, you can either downplay the event with them or come up with contingency plans to deal with the conflict.
- Separation: Another option is to try to keep conflicting attendees apart from each other in lodging location, teams, seating arrangements, etc.
- Lay down your weapons: Any items or topics that are likely to result in conflict should be banned. This can be a family heirloom that is in dispute or it could be a disagreement over politics, a common relative, property rights, etc.

In-Laws and Out-Laws
Sometimes conflicts are more likely when in-laws (a relative by marriage) and out-laws (a previous relative who is no longer one due to divorce) are involved. These can be challenging as they are not relatives by blood and may not have known the blood relatives as long. Also we are more likely to tolerate blood relatives than non-blood relatives.

The best way to handle or avoid conflict with these type of relationships may be to have team-building activities to help blood and non-blood relatives together. This may include having everyone give a short talk on their history, their goals, and what makes them tick. Data has shown that sometimes the more we know about someone and get to interact with them, the more likely we are able to get along with them. It doesn't always work out that way but, it's worthwhile trying it.

It can be particularly challenging for out-laws. You may run into this if a family member's ex-spouse is in attendance because the family member and ex have children together. If the family member and their ex don't get along well, you may want to pull that family member aside to see if there are any issues there that can be managed so as to not cause conflict.

Reunion Code of Conduct

It's always a good idea to set down a code of conduct or "rules of engagement" for your reunion. You may remember these from your school or work. These rules will communicate acceptable and unacceptable behavior. They can also provide direction on the use and scheduling of common areas and incorporate any rules associated with the lodging location.

Appendix B provides a sample code of conduct listing some rules that may apply to your event.

Section 1

Orientation

Before You Go

Before you leave for your family reunion, you need to do two things:

- Make sure you have taken care of everything you need to do prior to the reunion and making sure you have everything you need to bring to the reunion
- Provide any pre-arrival information to reunion attendees that they may need prior to departure.

It is beneficial to have checklists for both of the above.

A Reunion Planning Checklist identifies the key planning tasks that must be complete for the reunion and identify the key items to bring to the reunion.

A Vacation Travel Checklist is useful for any type of vacation, not just family reunions, but it is of particular value for family reunions as some family members have to remember to bring items needed for the reunion and not just for their own usage.

Appendix C has sample checklists for each of the above. These lists would need to be edited to include items that are unique to you and/or your family.

On-Site Preparations and Set-Up

Ideally, the reunion planning team members should arrive at the reunion location a day prior to the regular attendees. That way you will be able to set things up so everything is ready when the full crew arrives.

If getting there a day before is not an option, team members should try to arrive as early as possible on the start day of the reunion. If there isn't enough time to have the full orientation on the start day, you need to at least have a registration process so participants can receive anything they will need on that first day. You could then finish the orientation on the second day of the event.

If you have reserved a conference room for the orientation, make sure you call ahead the day before to make sure everything is in place and ready for your event. You will also want to check in when you first arrive to receive and give any last-minute directions to the facility host.

If you are having the orientation in a lodging unit, more than likely the orientation will occur early to late evening as you generally can't check into your unit until around 4 p.m. (which is why it's a good idea to arrive a day prior to the start of the event).

Don't forget to check on any auxiliary items you may need (tables, chairs, projectors, snacks, etc.).

Registration

You will want to have a formal or informal registration process where attendees can collect their reunion materials and received direction on any first-day activities or requirements. This can also be the time where you collect any monies due from participants.

You will need to set up an area in the main unit identified to hold activities or a conference room if you have reserved one. The planning team members would be responsible for manning the handout areas and providing information to attendees as needed.

The types of material to hand out may include:

- Guest book sign-in
- Name tags
- Orientation package

Meeting Places

You can't have a reunion if you don't have a place to meet and you need to plan carefully on your meeting locations!

To make sure that you account for all your get-togethers, list all your group meet-ups and identify the location/facilities for each meet-up (both indoor and outdoor). It's also a good idea to list all the auxiliary equipment you will need for your gathering as well as some logistical information. Some example meet-up information is below:

Family Reunion Meet-Up Information				
Activity	Location	Facility Reserved?	Auxiliary Equipment	Logistics/Notes
Orientation	Conference room	Yes	Computer, O/H projector	Bring gift bags
Picnic	Park	No	Tent, chairs, tablecloths	Part in Lot A
Whale Watching Cruise	Whale Watch Cabo	Yes	Binoculars, sunglasses	Arrive 30 mins early
⋮	⋮	⋮	⋮	⋮
⋮	⋮	⋮	⋮	⋮
⋮	⋮	⋮	⋮	⋮

Note the meeting places can change, so make sure to update your information and notify everyone of any changes as necessary.

Resort Layout

It's always a good idea to provide reunion attendees with the layout of your main reunion site. Whether you are having your event at a resort, campgrounds, or hotel, providing them with the lay of the land helps everybody get acclimated quickly and minimizes the confusion people may have in getting to their intended location.

You can usually obtain the site layout from the facility, on the Internet, or a third-party information site. For exterior layouts, you also may be able to use Google Maps or another mapping site to see how facilities are laid out.

These layouts normally show the locations of swimming pool(s), on-site restaurants, gyms, playgrounds, tennis courts, and so on.

If attendees are located in multiple locations, you will need to include all location layouts. In this case I also like to include a Google Map, which includes all the locations so attendees know where they are located relative to other attendee locations.

Location

THE LANGERHANS NOW UNDERSTOOD WHY THIS ISLAND WAS SUCH A CHEAP VACATION DESTINATION.

When the Wise Men searched for the location where Jesus was born, they "saw his star in the east and followed it to Bethlehem" (Bible, New International Version 2011, Matthew 2). You won't have a star to follow and you can't shoot from the hip when deciding where and when your family reunion will take place. You need to plan ahead to ensure you select the perfect location for your event and to make sure you are able to confirm the best accommodations for your group.

The first step is to determine what type of experience you want (beach, mountains, retreat, etc.). The type of experience you are looking for may determine the time of year you will want to schedule your reunion.

It's no fun going to the beach in 30 degree weather, for example, so summer may be the best time for a beach vacation. But if your family wants to go snow skiing, 30 degree weather may be perfect.

Other considerations are the size and availability of your group as well as transportation costs. Some options to consider are discussed below.

Staycations
Staycations normally would not be an option for a 7-day family reunion because that would mean imply that the 7-day event would be taking place at someone's house and confined to most relatives living in the same vicinity.

Someone would have to have a pretty big house to have sleeping accommodations for more than a few relatives. I don't know about you but that's not my situation!

Staycations are usually only an option for immediate family situations with possibly a few other relatives. If you live in a popular vacation destination and are having a very small family reunion, this may work for you.

Local Area
A local area family reunion is somewhat similar to a staycation reunion except that lodging isn't at someone's house but at accommodations in the local area. Again, if there are lots of things to do in your local area, this would work the same as having your reunion in a different destination. Your transportation costs would just be much lower and if you forget something you can just go home and get it!

Out of Area
Having a family union out of the area where you live is the primary focus of this book, though the information is just as relevant for local area reunions. It just takes more planning when you are vacationing out of your local area (that's why you need this book! ☺).

If you have family reunion planning experience, maybe you can just use this book as reference material but if you are a family reunion planning novice, you will what to treat this book as your bible when planning your family reunion.

Take your time when planning an extended family reunion out of your immediate area and remember to start your planning well in advance.

The rest of this section goes over some of the options you may want to consider when figuring out what location you want for your family reunion.

Attractions

Many people plan their family reunions around a key attraction such as Disney World, skiing, national parks, and so on. If this is you, this narrows down the potential location of your family reunion.

Once you have made the decision to align your reunion with a particular attraction, you only have to look for accommodations conveniently located in close proximity to that attraction.

Appendix D lists some top tourist attractions in the USA as a reference on options to consider.

Beach

I have to say that I have vacationed in many types of situations from beaches, mountains, cruises and so on, but most of my vacations are at beach locations. I love walking on the beach, hearing the waves, and smelling the ocean air.

You will need to decide what type of location rocks your family's boat. If it ends up being the beach, that would only be the tip of the iceberg in your decision-making as you will need to decide which beach to lay your towel down on. One of the big factors in this decision is transportation costs. Those Caribbean beaches may look nice, but the airfare cost to get there may not be in the budget.

Time of year is another key factor in deciding where you want your beach vacation to be. If you are planning your reunion during the winter, those Northeast USA beaches may not sound that enticing. There are many more options for a beach location during the summer though, as the USA has many appealing beach destinations during the warmer months.

Generally, if you are planning a beach family reunion in the USA, you would focus on the geographic area where most family members live, for example, East Coast beaches if members live on the East Coast and West Coast beaches when most live on the West Coast, but your mileage may differ. You need to think about what is most important to your family and align that desire with the costs to get to that desired beach location.

USNEWS list the following beach locations as the best Family Beach Vacations in the US (Travel n.d.):

1. Outer Banks, NC

2. Destin, FL
3. Sanibel Island, FL
4. Maui, HI
5. Hilton Head Island, SC
6. Myrtle Beach, SC
7. Honolulu – Oahu, HI
8. Cape May, NJ
9. St. Augustine, FL
10. Cannon Beach, OR
11. Jekyll Island, GA
12. Rehoboth Beach, DE
13. Santa Barbara, CA
14. Sandy Neck Beach, MA
15. Monterey, CA

If you are interested in a Mexican family reunion, TripSavvy lists the following best beach locations for Family Vacations in Mexico (Plowright 2019):

1. Riviera Maya
2. Los Cabos
3. Puerto Vallarta
4. Cancun

And finally, Fodor's list the following Best Caribbean Islands for Family Travel (Johnson 2018):

1. Jamaica
2. Puerto Rico
3. Anguilla
4. Providenciales, Turks and Caicos
5. Aruba
6. Grand Cayman
7. Antigua
8. Curacao
9. Barbados
10. The Dominican Republic

Again, your mileage may differ, but the above are some options for you to consider for your *beachy* family reunion.

Lakefront

Lakefront reunions can be similar to beach reunions though lakefront-based reunions tend to be more tranquil. Though some lakes have beaches, they generally don't make waves like oceans. Also, lakefront accommodations tend more toward cabins and campsites, while beachfronts tend to be lined with hotels and resorts.

Travel + Leisure listed the following top locations for a lakefront vacation (Yogerst 2020):

1. Lake Champlain, New York and Vermont: Best for History
2. Lake Superior, Michigan, Minnesota, and Wisconsin: Best for Fishing
3. Crater Lake, Oregon: Best for Scuba Diving
4. Lake Winnebago, Wisconsin: Best for Windsurfing
5. Lake Kabetogama, Minnesota: Best for Kayak or Canoe Camping
6. Lake Clark, Alaska: Best for Wilderness Adventure
7. Lake Tahoe, California and Nevada: Best for Snow Sports
8. Lake Michigan, Wisconsin, Michigan, Indiana, and Illinois: Best for Beaches
9. Finger Lakes, New York: Best for Wine Tastings
10. Lake Powell, Utah and Arizona: Best for Desert House boating
11. Lake Havasu, Arizona: Best for Partying
12. Moosehead Lake, Maine: Best for Ice Sports
13. Walden Pond, Massachusetts: Best for Reflection
14. Yellowstone Lake, Wyoming: Best for Sailing
15. Table Rock, Missouri: Best for Music
16. Caddo Lake, Texas and Louisiana: Best for Bigfoot Searches and Sightings
17. Lake Chelan, Washington: Best for Hiking
18. Lake Charles, Louisiana: Best for Cajun Culture
19. Lake Washington, Washington: Best for Hydroplane Racing
20. Flathead Lake, Montana: Best for Horseback Riding
21. Lady Bird Lake, Texas: Best for Stand-up Paddle Boarding
22. Lake Oconee, Georgia: Best for Golf
23. Lake Erie, Ohio: Best for Bird-Watching
24. Lake Coeur d'Alene, Idaho: Best for Triathlons
25. Lake of the Ozarks, Missouri: Best for Pampering

As you can see, there are many options for lakefront-based family reunions. Keep in mind the time of year you will be having your reunion when deciding on a lakefront event, as the weather can have a major bearing on which location would be feasible during your time frame.

Mountain/Skiing

Oh, to smell the clear fresh mountain air!

John Denver sang of his "Rocky Mountain High" and Marvin Gaye & Tammi Terrell sang of "Ain't No Mountain High Enough to Keep Me from Getting to You." Having a mountain-based family reunion can be a religious experience.

The best times for reunions on a mountain are spring, summer, fall, and winter. There is something to do during all seasons up on the mountain. If snow skiing is your thing, then winter is the time to go to take advantage of the peak of the snow season. If hiking, fishing, and nature watching is your cup of tea, then try for the other seasons, with summer being the most popular time frame for these activities.

The Travel Channel lists the following 8 Astonishing Family Mountain Vacations (8 Astonishing Family Mountain Vacations n.d.):

1. Banff National Park
2. Acadia National Park
3. Stowe Mountain
4. Pike's Peak
5. Yosemite National Park
6. Great Smoky Mountains
7. Pisgah National Forest
8. Adirondack Park

A separate list of Best Summer Mountain Vacations for Families is (Best Summer Mountain Vacations For Families n.d.):

1. Acadia National Park: Bar Harbor, Maine
2. Adirondack Mountains: New York
3. Aspen, Colorado
4. Attitash Mountain: Bartlett, New Hampshire
5. Cedar Breaks, Utah
6. Copper Mountain, Colorado
7. Donner Lake, California
8. Eureka Springs, Arkansas
9. Fallen Leaf Lake, California
10. Gatlinburg, Tennessee
11. Jackson, Wyoming
12. Mammoth Mountain, California
13. Massanutten, Virginia
14. Mount Rainier, Washington
15. Nemacolin Woodlands: Farmington, Pennsylvania

16. Park City, Utah
17. Sun Valley, Idaho
18. Telluride, Colorado
19. Whitefish, Montana
20. Winter Park, Colorado

Cruise

Come on baby and cruise with me!

If cruising is good for lovers, maybe it's good for family vacations as well. With something for everyone on board and the ability to visit several different countries, what's not to like!

Deciding to go on a cruise for a family vacation makes things much easier for the vacation planner. From lodging and food to activities and entertainment, it's all at your disposal. You just need to decide what your family wants to partake in.

Though there are some expensive cruises out there, cruising can offer exceptional value when you consider that lodging, meals, and most activities are included. This makes budgeting much easier, as you will know upfront, to a high level of certainty, what everyone's cost will be (except for some optional costs family members may incur).

The biggest decision you need to make with a cruise vacation is what cruise line/ship and itinerary. One key question is, do you select the cruise line/ship first or the itinerary? To answer this question, you need to determine which is more important to your family group: the cruise ship or the itinerary/locations visited? Other factors to consider, which may drive you to a particular selection, are cost and port of departure.

I'm a big fan of surveys, so to determine answers to the above questions, you can send out a questionnaire to solicit feedback from family members. Be careful that you don't present too many options though; otherwise you will never close on a selection. So try to come up with a moderate number of options for people to consider. Factors to consider are:

- Travel costs for most family members to get to the departure port
- Cruise stops of interest
- Cruise ship activities of interest
- Ship cabin sizes (max people per cabin type, etc.)
- Cost of cruise

The first thing you do is to filter the list down to only the ones that are within the budget for all attendees. This will reduce the number of options considerably.

For example, if most family members live on the East Coast, you may want to confine your options to cruises departing out of an East Coast port and if family members are on the West Coast, consider West Coast ports.

Cruise Ship Port Locations

Cruise ports are located in many coastal locations in the US, with destinations throughout the world. Costs can range from a few hundred dollars for a long weekend to thousands of dollars for luxury accommodations and exotic locations.

The options are too numerous to list all the amenities and experiences. You need to think about the key experiences you are looking for and always keep your budget in mind.

Cruise Lines

The number of cruise lines you have to choose from is a little more manageable than the number of destinations you can select. The major companies operating out of the US are below:

Major US Cruise Lines			
Cruise Line	**Headquarters**	**Telephone Number**	**Web Address**
Carnival Cruise Line	Doral, Florida	1-800-764-7419	https://www.carnival.com/#
Celebrity Cruises	Miami, Florida	1-800-647-2251	https://www.celebritycruises.com/
Costa Cruises	Owned by Carnival	1-800-462-6782	https://www.costacruises.com/
Disney Cruise Line	Celebration, Florida	1-800-951-3532	https://disneycruise.disney.go.com/
Holland America Line	Seattle, Washington	1-877-932-4259	https://www.hollandamerica.com/en_US.html
MSC Cruises	Geneva, Switzerland	1-877-665-4655	https://www.msccruisesusa.com/
Norwegian Cruise Line	Miami, Florida	1-866-234-0292	https://www.ncl.com/
Princess Cruises	Santa Clarita, California	1-800-774-6237	https://www.princess.com/
Royal Caribbean Cruise Line	Miami, Florida	1-866-562-7625	https://www.royalcaribbean.com/

More details on cruise port locations and destinations is provided in appendix E.

More information on recommended cruise lines is provided in appendix F.

Noroviruses on Cruise Ships

There has been a number of cases of acute gastrointestinal illnesses such as norovirus on cruise ships in the past. The frequency of these viruses is relatively low though. When present, these viruses can cause your stomach or intestines to get inflamed, causing you to have stomach pain, nausea, and diarrhea.

COVID-19 has caused additional concerns about cruising. As of this writing, cruises have been suspended until COVID-19 has come under control.

If you have any concerns about contracting any type of virus on cruise ships, you can contact your cruise line directly and/or check the following sites for additional information:

- CDC Facts About Noroviruses on Cruise Ships (Centers for Disease Control and Prevention 2018)
- CDC COVID-19 and Cruise Ship Travel (Centers for Disease Control and Prevention 2021)

Transportation

In order to start enjoying your family reunion, you need to get there. How you get there is the subject of this section. Of course, the distance you have to travel dictates which mode of transportation you will use. More than likely, family members will be coming from multiple locations so multiple transportation modes will likely be used. Are we there yet! ☺

Car

The great American vacations of the past almost all took place in the family car. Many family reunions were held close to home, making them more conducive to using cars as the mode of transportation. The few family members who dared to move farther away had to live with the realization that they would need to drive further to participant in the annual or biannual family reunions.

Having family reunions at drive-to locations for most family members is still popular though and is increasing in popularity given the cost of public transportation modes.

The Family Reunion Bible

Utilizing cars for reunions makes sense when traveling in groups of four or less, depending on the distance to your destination. You will need to determine how far is too far to drive for family members opting to use their car for transportation.

Normally when you are deciding on a family reunion location, you will consider how many family members will need to drive and have some idea of what their maximum driving distance is.

Bus

Not many people take the bus these days for family reunions but it can be an inexpensive mode of transportation. It may be an option for those who don't want to drive. Many of these buses have televisions and comfortable chairs, providing a less stressful trip. You can also take advantage of group rates.

Many public bus companies can transport your group to many vacation destinations throughout the US. Some can even take you to Canada and Mexico from US stations. There are also some Mexican bus companies that can pick you up and transport you to Mexican destinations.

You may be surprised to know that there are also bus charter companies that have special charters geared toward family reunions. Don't forget to leave these out if you are considering using buses as your preferred means of transport to your reunion destination.

Appendix G provides some useful information on different bus companies to consider for your reunion.

Train

The train is not a viable option for large group travel because of the expense (maybe except for the well-heeled), but a small immediate family group may consider it for transportation to their family reunion. Generally though, you would need to plan on departing at least one day prior to the reunion start date as train travel can take some time.

The options for long-distance train transportation are slim (Amtrak anyone?). Amtrak is the only reasonable game in town in the US, but you can get to anywhere in the country over its extensive network.

Cost
Amtrak tickets are generally higher than traveling by air if you book a roomette or

bedroom (though the price does include meals), but their coach seats are sometimes cheaper than coach seats on an airplane. You would need to purchase well in advance though, as prices usually rise as seats are reserved.

Comfort

Before I took my trip on Amtrak, I had read that the coach seats inclined and were very comfortable. That wasn't my experience! They were OK for sitting, but sleeping on them, for adults, could not be considered comfortable. To make the best of it, if you must purchase coach seats, bring your own pillows and blankets and know that you are going to be a little stiff when you wake up.

For a more comfortable overnight trip, you can purchase a sleeping compartment. Amtrak offers the following different ticket options:

- Coach: Just a seat
- Roomette: Two comfortable seats by day and upper and lower berths by night
- Bedroom: Twice the space of a roomette and features a sofa and armchair by day and upper and lower berths by night
- Bedroom Suite: Combine two adjoining bedrooms
- Family Bedroom: Span the width of a car with ample space for two adults and two children (aged 2–12). Features two sofas by day and two upper and two lower berths by night
- Accessible Bedroom: Located on the entry level of the train and offers ample space for a wheelchair. Each room features a sofa for two by day and upper and lower berths by night.

Famous American Train Routes

There are some famous train routes you can take advantage of if your travels coincide with certain destinations. Those routes are as follows:

- ➤ The Coast Starlight: Seattle – Portland – Sacramento – Los Angeles (35 hours)
- ➤ The Southwest Chief: Chicago – Kansas City – Albuquerque – Flagstaff – Los Angeles (40+ hours)
- ➤ California Zephyr: Chicago – Omaha – Denver – Salt Lake City – Emeryville (San Francisco) (51+ hours)
- ➤ Capitol Limited: Washington, DC – Pittsburgh – Cleveland – Chicago (18 hours)
- ➤ Empire Builder: Chicago – St. Paul/Minneapolis – Spokane – Portland/Seattle (46 hours)

> City of New Orleans: Chicago – Memphis – New Orleans (19 hours)

Auto Train
If you happen to be traveling by train from the Washington, DC/Northern Virginia area to the Orlando, Florida, area you can take advantage of Amtrak's Auto Train. Some people living as far north as New York and New England drive down to the DC area to take the car train to Florida.

The Auto Train allows you to take your car and all occupants in the car on the train. There is a separate charge for the car and each occupant. The Auto Train is the only one of its kind in the United States. It operates between Lorton, Virginia, (20 miles outside of Washington, DC) and Sanford, Florida (25 miles outside of Orlando, Florida) with no stops. Coach fares are as low as $89 per person plus the cost of your vehicle.

The train departs around 4 p.m. and arrives around 9 a.m. the next day from both locations. The seating/sleeping options are the same as with other Amtrak trains. The luggage in your car stays in your car so you don't have to move your luggage.

At departure time you drive your car up to a staging area where it is driven into the car by an Amtrak employee. On arrival another Amtrak employee drives your car off the train. You then enter your car and drive away to your final destination.

If you have the time and live in the Washington, DC/Northern Virginia area or points north, you may want to consider taking advantage of the Auto Train at least once to experience it for yourself.

Airplane
The final transportation option is the airplane. Air transportation usually costs the most, but in many cases it is the only rational option. There are a number of steps you can take to minimize your airfare costs, including the following:

Timing
Timing is everything when it comes to determining when you should purchase your airline tickets. FareCompare lists the following strategies to reduce the cost of airline tickets (Seaney 2019):

1. Shop on Tuesday: Best day to shop
2. Don't Shop too Early or too Late
    a. US Tickets – Shop between 3 months and 30 days before departure
    b. International Tickets – Shop between 5½ months and 1½ months before departure

3. Always Compare Airfare
4. Cheapest Days to Fly
    a. US Tickets – Tuesday, Wednesday and Saturday
    b. International Tickets – Weekdays
    c. Cheap Times of Day – Dawn overnight, lunch & dinner hours
5. Fly the Cheapest Route
6. Book Group Travel One Ticket at a Time

Frequent Flyer Tickets

If you normally fly on a particular airline, it may pay to take advantage of reserving tickets with frequent flyer points. Most airlines have a frequent flyer program that allows you to earn frequent flyer points for air travel on that airline as well as with purchases with partners of that airline. The reasons to join a frequent flyer program are to earn:

- Free flights
- Seat upgrades
- Elite status
- Free checked bags
- Priority check-in and boarding

A comparison of the airline frequent flyer programs is presented in the following table:

U. S. Airline Frequent Flyer Programs							
		Points		Elite Status Min. Reqmts.~			
Airline Name	Program Name	Per Flight Miles	Approx. Value per Point^	Miles/ Points	Segments	Spend*	Do Miles Expire?
Alaska Airlines	Mileage Plan	1.0	1.0 cent	20,000	NA	NA	Yes
American Airlines	Aadvantage	5 per dollar	1.0 cent	25,000	30	$3,000	Yes
Delta Air Lines	SkyMiles	5 per dollar	0.9 cent	25,000	30	$3,000	No
Frontier Airlines	frontier Miles	1.0	0.3 cent	20,000	NA	NA	Yes
Hawaiian airlines	HawaiianMiles	1.0	1.1 cents	20,000	30	NA	Yes
JetBlue Airways	TrueBlue	3 per dollar	1.1 cents	12,000	30	NA	No
Southwest Airlines	Rapid Rewards	6 per dollar	1.6 cents	35,000	25	NA	No
Spirit Airlines	Free Spirit	6 per dollar	NA	2,000	NA	NA	Yes
Sun Country Airlines	Country Rewards	2 per dollar	NA	Discontinued			Yes
United Airlines	MileagePlus	5 times fare	1.0 cent	25,000	30	$3,000	No

^Nerdwallet.com (Kemmis 2021)
*US residents only
~Per year

Airline Credit Cards

Another method of securing airline miles is with airline credit cards. Many airlines have them and they usually offer a sign-up bonus of free frequent flyer points.

The Family Reunion Bible

If you have a favorite airline you primarily fly with, it may be beneficial to secure that airlines' credit card. As with all credit cards though, watch out for high-interest rates and if you are not paying off your balances every month, the cost of owning these credit cards may be higher than the value you receive from their frequent flyer miles.

Some airline credit cards that give you frequent flyer points based on your purchases follows:

Airline Credit Cards Giving Frequent Flyer Miles				
Airline	Miles Card	Annual Fee*	Regular APR*	Miles per Dollar Spent*
Alaska Airlines	Visa Signature Credit Card	$75	15.99%-23.99%	Up to 3.0
American Airlines	Aadvantage MileUp℠ Card	$0	15.99%-24.99%	2.0
British Airways	Visa Signature® Card	$95	15.99%-22.99%	Up to 5.0
Delta	SkyMiles® Blue American Express Card	$0	15.74%-24.74%	Up to 2.0
Delta	SkyMiles® Gold American Express Card	$99	15.74%-24.74%	Up to 2.0
Delta	SkyMiles® Platinum American Express Card	$250	15.74%-24.74%	Up to 3.0
Delta	SkyMiles® Reserve American Express Card	$550	15.74%-24.74%	Up to 3.0
JetBlue	Plus Card	$99	15.99%-24.99%	Up to 6.0
Southwest Airlines	Rapid Rewards® Performance Business Credit Card	$199	15.99%-22.99%	Up to 3.0
Southwest Airlines	Rapid Rewards® Plus Credit Card	$69	15.99%-22.99%	Up to 2.0
Southwest Airlines	Rapid Rewards® Premier Credit Card	$99	15.99%-22.99%	Up to 2.0
Southwest Airlines	Rapid Rewards® Priority Credit Card	$149	15.99%-22.99%	Up to 2.0
United Airlines	Explorer Card	$95	16.49%-23.49%	Up to 2.0
United Airlines	Gateway℠ Card	$0	16.49%-23.49%	Up to 3.0

*Annual Fees, APR and miles can change so check card for current values

Non-Airline Credit Cards

Sometimes non-airline credit cards are a better value than airline credit cards because you may be able to use these cards to secure frequent flyer points from multiple airlines.

Some of the non-airline credit cards that give you frequent flyer points based on your purchases follows:

Non-Airline Credit Cards Giving Frequent Flyer Miles				
Credit Card Company	Miles Card	Annual Fee*	Regular APR*	Miles per Dollar Spent*
American Express	Gold Card	$250	15.99%-22.99%	Up to 4.0
	The Platinum Card®	$550	15.99%-22.99%	Up to 10.0
Bank of america	Premium Rewards® Credit Card	$95	15.99%-22.99%	Up to 2.0
	Travel Rewards Credit Card	$0	14.99%-22.99%	1.5
Capital One	Venture Rewards Credit Card	$95	17.24%-24.49%	2.0
	VentureOne Rewards Credit Card	$0	15.49%-25.49%	1.25
Chase	Sapphire Preferred® Card	$95	15.99%-22.99%	Up to 2.0
Citi	Aadvantage® Executive World Elite Mastercard®	$450	15.99%-24.99%	Up to 2.0
	Aadvantage® Platinum Select® World Elite Mastercard®	$99	15.99%-24.99%	2.0
	CitiBusiness® Aadvantage® Platinum Select® Mastercard®	$99	15.99%-24.99%	Up to 2.0
	Premier® Card	$95	15.99%-23.99%	Up to 3.0
Discover	Discover It® Miles	$0	11.99%-22.99%	1.5
U.S. Bank	Altitude® Go Visa Signature® Card	$0	14.99%-23.99%	Up to 4.0
Wells Fargo	Propel American Express® Card	$0	14.49%-24.99%	Up to 3.0

*Annual Fees, APR and miles can change so check card for current values

Lodging

Once you have selected the location for your vacation, you will need to decide on the accommodations. *The early bird gets the worm* with respect to lodging. You don't want to wait so late to select your lodging that you end up staying in a manger like Jesus! Before you say *"what was good enough for Jesus is good enough for me,"* keep in mind that a manger was not the first choice for Jesus's parents, Joseph and Mary. They had to stay in a manger because all the other accommodations were full. Don't let that be your fate.

The type of lodging you select for your vacation is very important, and when you are planning an extended vacation it becomes even more important. You have to consider the needs and desires of all the people who will be attending. Some people may be content to pitch a tent on a campground and they are good, but that type of rustic living may not appeal to the masses. On the other end of the spectrum, some members may be used to the Ritz Carlton life but those prices may be a little too high for everybody. In general, you want to focus on pricing somewhere in between these two extreme options.

Available amenities will play an important part in what type of lodging you decide on. Some of the common amenities to consider near or on-property are:

- Activities/activity center
- Banquet/conference room
- Biking trails
- Beach
- Childcare/kids club
- Exercise room / fitness center
- Game room
- Golf
- Fishing
- Hiking trails
- Lake
- Laundry facilities
- Parking
- Playground
- Restaurants & bars
- Shopping: gift shop, clothing boutique, etc.
- Spa
- Sports courts: basketball, tennis, volleyball, etc.
- Swimming pool
- Wedding services (if a wedding will be involved)
- Wi-Fi/Internet service

Extended vacations with large groups tend to work better with condo-type accommodations with kitchens. These give you a lot of flexibility and space to save money and to make everybody comfortable. With that in mind, below are some common options for lodging in ascending order of preference.

Campgrounds/Cabins

Campgrounds and cabins can be a reasonable family reunion option for those families who like to keep it simple, inexpensive, and who enjoy the outdoors. Some family members may be diehard campers who get excited about getting back to nature and surviving the way the original Native Americans lived, while other members may prefer to view their nature from a penthouse balcony on Park Avenue! You will need to select a site that will be a reasonable compromise that everyone can live with.

So if camping will be your reunion abode, some key considerations are:

- Campsite location
- Type of Accommodations
- Site Amenities
- Available On-site/Nearby Activities

Campsite Location

Family reunion locations were discussed earlier in this section, so the additional research you need to perform when selecting a location is to identify locations which campsites and/or cabins in the area.

One of the oldest and well-known organizations providing information on camping throughout North America is KOA (koa 2021). Go to their website and click on "Find a Campground" at the top of the page to find information on all their affiliated camping sites.

The United States National Park Service (NPS) also provides a resource for finding NPS campgrounds on their website (National Park Service 2020). This site provides you with information on why you should camp, how to camp, and how to stay safe, among other useful information.

Travel + Leisure lists "24 of the Most Scenic Places to Camp in the United States" (Romano 2020).

For the more discerning camper, Conde Nast Traveler lists "The Best Place to Camp in Every State" (Pennington 2020).

Type of Accommodations

You have several common types of camping accommodations to select from for your reunion:

1. Tent spaces
2. RV sites
3. Basic cabins
4. Deluxe cabins

On top of these, you can add more unique accommodations, such as:

1. Teepees
2. Airstream and vintage trailers
3. Cabooses
4. Treehouses
5. Western-style wagons
6. Yurts

Section 1

Site Amenities

You will want to consider the available amenities present at your campsite. Some popular amenities are:

- Customer service in case of issues
- Drinking water
- Electrical service
- Firepit
- Gas grills
- Hot tub
- Lake or river
- Movie nights
- Pets allowed
- Picnic area
- RV hookups
- Showers
- Toilets/bathrooms
- Vending machines
- Wi-Fi service

Available Activities

It's not a reunion if there are no activities! Some common activities you may find at campsites are:

- Bike trail
- Bird-watching
- Campfire storytelling
- Fishing
- Food trucks
- Hiking
- Nature walks
- Outdoor communal campground kitchens
- Stargazing
- S'more making
- Swimming pools
- Zip line

Hotels/Resorts

Hotels and resort hotels are a major mainstay for family reunion lodging. They are available everywhere, allowing you unlimited choices when selecting a reunion location.

You will usually tend more toward resort-type hotels for your event as they generally provide more amenities and activities of interest for family reunions.

Hotels and resorts generally come with a higher cost than other types of accommodations, so you will need to do your research to keep the costs down while achieving the level of luxury you can live with.

Not to recreate the wheel, below are some useful references to consider for hotel/resort reunion lodging:

- Family Destinations Guide's "15 Best Family Reunion Resorts, Places, & Venues – Everyone Will Love" (Reeve 2020).
- Family Vacation Critic's "12 Best Resorts for Family Reunions" (Stapen 2019).
- Taste of Home's "The Best Family Reunion Spot in Every State" (Mattison 2019).
- Oyster's "The Best Hotels for Family reunions in the US" (Grant 2017).
- Travel + Leisure's "Best Resorts for Family Reunions" (Goran 2009).
- Trips to Discover's "9 Budget Resorts for Family Reunions" (Wofford 2019).

Rental Condos

Rental condos are a less expensive option than hotels/resorts for family reunion lodging. In many cases you are able to reserve a multi-bedroom condo for the price of a single hotel room. Condos generally come with a full kitchen, living room, bathrooms, and all the amenities normally associated with a condo. In addition, many condos come with resort-style amenities such as swimming pools, gym, and so on.

The big dogs in the United States for condo rentals are Airbnb, FlipKey, and VRBO. A more complete list of condo rental sites follows:

Major Short-term Condo Rental Sites		
Site Name	Site Summary	Website
Airbnb	Marketplace for vacation rentals and tourism activities.	https://www.airbnb.com/
Expedia	Good for combining with car rentals and flights.	https://www.expedia.com/
FlipKey	Tripadvisor condo rental site.	https://www.flipkey.com/
Getaway	For those looking to escape and embrace nature.	https://getaway.house/
HomeToGo	World's largest vacation rental search engine.	https://www.hometogo.com/
HouseTrip	"The Airbnb of Europe" (owned by Tripadvisor).	https://www.housetrip.com/
Luxury Retreats	Airbnb's luxury vacation options.	https://www.airbnb.com/luxury
Marriott Homes & Villas	If you want to splurge.	https://homes-and-villas.marriott.com/
OneFineStay	Luxury option for travelers seeking a five-star experience.	https://www.onefinestay.com/
Outdoorsy	RV, camper van, and travel trailer rentals.	https://www.outdoorsy.com/
Plum Guide	For those who prefer only the best of the best.	https://www.plumguide.com/
Sonder	Best for big city vacations.	https://www.sonder.com/
Tripping	A leading search engine for vacation rentals	https://www.tripping.com/
TurnKey	Best for hotel-level service.	https://www.turnkeyvr.com/
VRBO	American vacation rental online marketplace.	https://www.vrbo.com/
Wimdu	One of the world's leading search engines for vacation rentals.	https://www.wimdu.com/

Note that many of the above sites charge an additional servicing fee that is only displayed when you start the booking process.

Timeshares

A timeshare is a vacation property with shared ownership. A management company handles the construction and sells shares, which entitles buyers to spend a specified amount of time (usually one week per year) at the property. Some timeshares are large complexes with dozens of living units, while others resemble a single-family home and are only large enough for one owner to occupy at a time. Most timeshares are located in popular resort areas where vacation property is in high demand.

Renting timeshare(s) directly from an owner for your family reunion can be less expensive than other resort options, as timeshares are usually condos set in a resort-style atmosphere. As a matter of fact, many of the condos advertised on the above condo rental sites are timeshare units being rented by owners.

If any family members own timeshares, they may be able to secure units for all participants through the use of their ownership and the various exchange opportunities available to timeshare owners. The different options available to timeshare owners for exchanging and acquiring extra vacation weeks are outside the scope of this book but if you have timeshare owners in your group, they will be able to provide you with some of the options at their disposal.

Timeshares are available in most locations you would consider for your reunion, including beach, mountain, and lake locations, as well as locations convenient to major attractions.

Many major hotel and resort development companies also have timeshare divisions, including the following ones:

- Bluegreen
- Diamond
- Disney
- Hilton
- Hyatt
- Marriott
- Shell
- Westin/Sheraton
- WorldMark
- Wyndham

Besides the list of short-term condo rental sites listed above, you can rent timeshares on the following sites:

Section 1

Timeshare Rental Sites			
Site Name	**Site Summary**	**Fee***	**Website**
Craigslist	Search for "vacation	None	www.craigslist.com
Ebay	Timeshare rental category.	None	https://www.ebay.com/sch/i.html?_from=R40&_trksid=p2380057.m570.l2632&_nkw=timeshare+rental&_sacat=16123
KOALA	Goal is to make it easier for travelers to rent timeshares at beautiful resorts.	$0.05	https://www.go-koala.com/
MVC Rentals	Marriott timeshare rental site.	None	https://mvcrentals.marriott.com
My Resort Network	Provides a network for timeshare owners to rent their weeks.	None	https://www.myresortnetwork.com/
Redweek	Largest online timeshare marketplace.	$18.99	https://www.redweek.com/
SMTN	Features rent by owner timeshare vacation	None	https://www.sellmytimesharenow.com/timeshare-rentals/
Timeshare Rentals & Sales	Select author timeshare rentals and sales.	None	https://thomasinfoweb.com/timeshare-rentals-sales/
TS Today	Timeshare magazone subscription including timeshare rental ads.	$29.00	https://timesharingtoday.com/
TUG	Timeshare rentals	None	https://tug2.com/timeshare-rentals/default.aspx

*Per year

To show you the value of renting timeshares for your group reunion, I have selected several resorts to compare the cost of renting those units directly from the resort versus renting them from a timeshare owner (see appendix H).

Food/Meals

> "Then God said, I give you every seed-bearing plant on the face of the whole earth and every tree that has fruit with seed in it. They will be yours for food" (Genesis n.d., 1:29).

Many people have the attitude that they don't want to cook when they are on vacation. If that is your family, your options for food become fairly straightforward, you will be doing a lot of eating out. Eating out becomes quite expensive though for a family reunion. Plus, some family members may not be able to afford the extravagance of eating out all the time. In addition, some participants may have certain food restrictions that may make it easier if they prepared their own meals.

Most families will do a combination of cooking and eating out during their reunions. Some of the options at your disposal are listed in this section.

All-Inclusive

Many hotels/resorts offer all-inclusive meal plans to their guests. These plans normally include all meals as well as some services and activities such as Internet service, access to gyms, transportation to the facility from the airport, and so on. Generally, everyone in your lodging unit would have to select all-inclusive to participate. Often you have to select this option for your full stay but sometimes you can also select a shorter period such as for three days (though the shorter period has to be consecutive days).

These plans can be quite expensive but they do make your meal planning simple. The costs are listed as per person per day and there may be different prices for adults and children. In addition, there may be both basic and deluxe plans where the deluxe plans include more expensive restaurants and/or more expensive alcoholic beverages.

> ✋Note that you can hear the term "European Plan." This term is mostly used in European countries and doesn't mean all-inclusive. "European Plan" means that only the hotel accommodations are included in the price. Meals or beverages may be available but for an additional fee.

Many people find that they can't eat enough food to justify paying for an all-inclusive plan unless they drink a lot of alcoholic beverages. If you want to perform a rough calculation to compare the per-person costs of the all-inclusive plan versus other meal options. You will need to make sure to include all the items included in the all-inclusive plan so you can perform an apples-to-apples comparison. A sample table you can complete is provided below:

Cost of All-inclusive Plan vs Other Meal Options					
Item Type	Item	Average Per-person Daily Cost		
		All-inclusive	Eating Out	Cooking
Meals & Beverages	Breakfast	Included		
	Lunch	Included		
	Dinner	Included		
	Non-alcoholic Beverages	Included		
	Alcholic Beverages	Included		
Activities	Entertainment	Included		
	Daily activities	Included		
	Water sports	Included		
	Gym	Included		
		Included		
Services	Shuttle to/from airport	Included		
	Spa Access/discount	Included		
	Late checkout	Included		
		Included		
		Included		
	Total Cost:			

Note that what's included in an all-inclusive plan varies from resort to resort, so you will need to find out what's included at your facility.

Some of the benefits and liabilities of selecting an all-inclusive plan are as follows:

Pros
- May cost less money
- Less use of credit card
- Less cash to carry

- Easier to keep to a budget
- Food available throughout the day
- Mostly everything is included
- Convenience
- Good for first-time travelers
- Included services and activities

Cons
- May cost more money
- Less authentic
- Limited opportunity to sample local food
- Less opportunity to explore
- More likely to gain weight
- Doesn't always mean *all-inclusive*
- Crowds/noise
- Noise
- Fine print (unexpected costs)

Eating Out

Eating out provides you with the most options for selecting your meals. But with this flexibility comes great responsibility! ☺

It takes a lot of planning to decide where to eat for a large group of people. Generally, you will need to make reservations for large groups unless you will be going to an all-you-can-eat buffet restaurant (you may want to make reservations for buffets also to ensure everyone in your party can be seated together).

Eating out all the time can also be very expensive, and don't forget the transportation costs to transport all reunion participants to and from the restaurant.

Eating out does allow you to sample some of the local cuisine in your local area and interact more with the locals. You may want to selectively eat out for a subset of your family reunion meals to keep costs down. Plan carefully though to get the most bang for your buck.

Eating In

Even though cooking in is not everyone's cup of tea, generally it will save you money compared to eating out or going with an all-inclusive meal plan. It does take time and work of course. You will need to go grocery shopping and you may end up with food and other purchases left over at the end of your reunion.

Many people bring some items from home (seasoning, special utensils, detergent, etc.) to save money and to avoid having to make bulk purchases for items in which you only need small amounts.

Many resorts will have small on-site grocery stores but the prices will be expensive and the selections will be limited. It's best to find a convenient larger grocery store to shop at even though you will have to travel to get to it.

Family reunion meals may consist of each immediate family group cooking their own meals or meals are jointly prepared by all reunion participants together.

Meals prepared by the whole group take on the form of a *potluck* or *cooperative cooking*:

- Potluck – A communal gathering where each guest or group contributes a different, often homemade, dish of food to be shared.
- Cooperative cooking – you exchange quantities of a food staple or meal and in return you get another different staple or meal.

For a potluck, each immediate family group prepares enough of one or more food items to feed the whole group and everybody eats together. Often you would include some other activity while everyone is together, including games, entertainment, and so on.

Cooperative cooking is similar to a potluck but people don't necessarily have to eat together and the number of people and meals is more limited.

For both potlucks and cooperative cooking, you need to keep in mind any food allergies or other food restrictions any of your family members have. If you are not able to exclude all of these types of items, you need to make sure they are clearly labeled and kept away from members who may have an adverse reaction to them.

Meal Kit Delivery Services

If you want to make your cooking in easier, you may want to take advantage of one of the Meal Kit delivery services available at your family reunion location. These kits make your cooking experience easier by providing the food (in the correct portions), seasonings, and easy recipes to cook your own meals. They can deliver daily or weekly menus and proportioned ingredients to those who would like to cook their own meals to save money but they don't want to take the time to go purchase the food and figure out how to cook it.

Some of the meal kit delivery services available in the United States are as follows:

United States Meal Kit Services (Dinner)			
Service Name	Service Areas*	Min. Order Per Week	Website
Blue Apron	Nationwide	$60	https://www.blueapron.com/
Crowd Cow	Everywhere in the U.S., except Hawaii and Alaska	$65 to $140	https://www.crowdcow.com/
Daily Harvest	95% of the continental U.S.	$70	https://www.daily-harvest.com/
Dinnerly	Ships to most of the West Coast, Midwest, and Southern states	$39	https://dinnerly.com/
EveryPlate	Most of the continental U.S.	$39	https://www.everyplate.com/
Factor	Ships to every state except Hawaii and Alaska	$60	https://www.factor75.com/r/home
Fresh & Easy	Nationwide	$35	https://www.freshandeasy.com/
FreshDirect	New York city, New Jersey, Connecticut, Pennsylvania, Delaware, Washington D.C.	$30	https://www.freshdirect.com/
Freshly	Nationwide	$46	https://www.freshly.com/
Fresh n' Lean	Nationwide	$8	https://www.freshnlean.com/
Gobble	Continental U.S.	$56	https://www.gobble.com/
Green Chef	All over the U.S., except for Alaska, Hawaii, and parts of Louisiana	$60	https://www.greenchef.com
HelloFresh	Nationwide and abroad	$60	https://www.hellofresh.com/
Home Chef	98% of the country	$45	https://www.homechef.com/
Hungryroot	Most zip codes in the 48 contiguous states and Washington D.C.	$67	https://www.hungryroot.com/
Martha & Marley Spoon	Most of the continental U.S.	$18	https://marleyspoon.com/
Purple Carrot	Ships to most zip codes in the U.S., excluding Alaska and Hawaii	$72	https://www.purplecarrot.com/
Sakara Life	Nationwide	$80	https://www.sakara.com/
Snap Kitchen	Free delivery within a specific zone and pick up from 35+ shops located throughout Austin, Dallas, Houston, and Philadelphia	$25	https://www.snapkitchen.com/
Splendid Spoon	All over the U.S., except for Alaska and Hawaii	$65	https://splendidspoon.com/
Sunbasket	Most zip codes in the United States, excluding Alaska, Hawaii, Montana, and parts of New Mexico	$72	https://sunbasket.com/
Veestro	All contiguous 48 states	$30	https://www.veestro.com/
Yumbles	Most of the East Coast, Texas, and parts of the West Coast and Midwest, with plans to expand nationwide	$30	https://www.yumbles.com/

*As of March 2021

> ☚ Note that many of these meal kit services require a monthly subscription, and if they don't, you will need to order well ahead of your reunion date to ensure the meals arrive in time (there may also be a delivery charge).

Catered Meals

Eating in does not necessarily mean you have to cook. An option for some meals is to have them catered. This is different from an all-inclusive plan as the cost of a catered meal is a function of the number of people, and you can cater as few or as many meals as you like.

Also, you aren't limited to the resort services when selecting who you want to cater your meals. You generally have the ability to have your meals catered by outside companies.

In the United States, many restaurants and grocery stores provide food catering services directly to their customers. Some restaurants also provide this service via a third party, such as Grubhub, DoorDash, Uber Eats, and so on.

There are also independent food catering businesses. You will need to check your local area for a list of these companies.

Section 1

Activities

> **The only worthwhile thing for a human being is to eat, drink, and enjoy life's goodness that he finds in what he accomplishes. This, I observed, is also from the hand of God himself.** (Bible, New International Version 2011, Ecclesiastes 2:24)

Meghan Trainor sang that it's "All About That Bass" (Trainor 2014). I say it's all about vacationing with family and enjoying activities together! From active pursuits to relaxing, it's all good. In this section we will be discussing some of the activities you may want to consider for your family reunion.

"MY NINE LIFE PRESERVERS ARE SUFFOCATING ME."

Relaxing

Don't forget the relaxing! During the first several family reunions I planned, our itinerary was packed solid with no time to go to the bathroom. I soon realized that part of the journey was to have time to smell the roses and relax. Whether that was lounging at the pool or beach or sleeping in, it's important to take some time to reenergize by taking a moment. I list this activity first because I don't want you to forget!

Indoor Activities

Most of my indoor family gatherings have been in my unit as I always have a very large condo with big living room areas to accommodate everyone. This has worked for up to 40 people. If you have more than that or accommodations that can't handle that many you should reserve a conference room.

Your indoor activities may include indoor games, a start of reunion orientation meeting, pot luck meals, and so on. You also want to have a backup plan for some type of indoor activities in case of inclement weather.

Make sure you have a plan for how you will accommodate everyone for your indoor activities. If you are going to need a conference room, for example, make sure you select accommodations that have a room that will work for your family. Keep in mind that the size/capacity isn't the only thing you need to be concerned about. You need to make sure the facility has all the supplemental items you need, such as audio/video equipment, banquet tables, game tables, food preparation/delivery, and so on.

Also, make sure you have/bring all the items you need for your indoor events (games, playing cards, and so on). All these items should be listed on your checklist (you will have a checklist, right?).

Let's Get Acquainted

You will want to have some sort of get acquainted event. Particularly if family members will be there whom you don't see very often, if ever. This may include icebreaker activities, introductions, and an orientation.

This is something you would do early on during your week, preferably the first night or the first full day.

This can be an informal event, but you want to make sure you can accommodate everyone at the event location, and you will want to have refreshments and appetizers available. Include the cost for this in your budget if you think the cost will be high.

Attractions & Festivals

What's a vacation without an attraction/ festival or two (or three) to attend? You can't lay on the beach all day, can you?

I don't know about you but attending festivals and enjoying different attractions is a big thing for me. It's true that the focus of this book is planning and enjoying your family reunion, but you are also on vacation, so you may want to take advantage of all that your reunion locale has to offer.

If you have some flexibility in your event dates, you should research to see if any festivals or special events are occurring in your reunion location and tweak your reunion dates to coincide with the event. For example, if you are planning a June reunion and you are flexible on which June week, pick the one that has a special event taking place that your family members by be interested in attending.

> ✋ When scheduling reunion activities, make sure you don't schedule anything that conflicts with any special events taking place in the general area of your reunion.

Look for unique attractions near your reunion site that may be of interest to some family members and include that information in your reunion handouts. You may want to go to certain attractions with the whole reunion crew if it fits in with your reunion theme.

An added bonus is if an annual festival is taking place during your event. There are numerous types of festivals to choose from, including the following types:

- Arts and crafts
- Beer
- Culture, heritage and folk
- Film
- Flower
- Food and wine
- Holiday
- Music
- Pioneer
- Religious
- Renaissance
- Rodeo and horse racing
- Science
- Seasonal
- Sports
- Steampunk
- Storytelling

Pick and choose the ones to want to consider for your reunion. To help you along, I have provided a table of some popular US festivals in appendix I.

Cookbooks

If you have any closet chefs in your family, you may want to distribute a cookbook during your reunion. This requires preplanning though, as the book would need to be published and printed prior to the event. Some families will sell their cookbooks to use the proceeds to help fund their reunion.

If you are not able to have your cookbook available for your reunion, an alternate solution is to collect recipes at the reunion and publish the book after the event.

Family cookbooks are a good way to preserve those secret family recipes (though they won't be secret anymore!) and make them available to future generations of family members.

You will want a consistent look and feel for your cookbook, so you will need to create or purchase a template that participants can use to document their recipes. The key information needed for the recipes are:

- Name of the dish
- List of ingredients
- Directions for making the dish

It is always nice to include a picture of the dish after it has been made. For a family reunion cookbook, I would also add a picture of the cook!

After all of the recipes are collected, somebody has to create the book. If you are going for the lowest cost possible, you can just organize the recipes, add the front and back matter and staple the pages together, but I would not recommend that method. Self-publishing a book is relatively inexpensive these days and you will end up with a product that will last a long time.

How to publish a book is beyond the scope of this book, but some of the top self-publishing companies you can select from are:

- Amazon KDP
- BookBaby
- BookBub
- IngramSpark
- Kobo
- Lulu
- Smashwords

There are several more good ones as well. By using the above companies to publish your book, you can make it available for sale so it can be purchased directly without you having to deal with warehousing any books. Of course if you want to sell direct you can do that also. Make sure you price the book to cover all the printing costs plus an acceptable royalty (profit). Any net profits you receive can be reallocated to reunion expenses.

Escape Room

Escape rooms are a relatively new group activity. It is a game in which a group of people are put in a room and they have to discover clues, solve puzzles, and accomplish tasks in order to escape the room or multiple rooms (don't worry, if your family is mentally challenged and you get in and can't get out, you will be let out after a certain amount of time has elapsed). This could be a great way to bond with your family members to band together to solve a common goal.

If you have a large group, you may want to divide the group up into smaller groups and the subgroups can compete against each other to see who can escape the fastest.

There are numerous escape rooms throughout the United States and the world. One list of top USA rooms is Escape Room Services' "USA's Best Escape Rooms" (Escape The Roomz 2019).

Family History

Many people enjoy having a family history component of their family reunions. That makes sense considering that you will have a group of the family there and many people are interested in who their relatives and ancestors are.

There are two related aspects of family history research:

- Searching historical records residing in physical and online repositories
- DNA research

Record Search

The old-fashioned way of researching family history was to go to physical sites to search records in different archives. These archives included the following:

- Census records
- Birth, marriage and death records
- Cemetery records
- Church records
- City directories
- Court records
- Funeral home records

- Immigration and naturalization records
- Land records
- Military records
- Newspapers
- Oral histories
- Personal family history records and stories
- Photographs and scrapbooks
- Prison records
- Ship manifests/passenger lists
- Union records
- Wills and probate records

The above records could have been scattered all over the United States if your ancestors moved around a lot as each state and county kept their individual records.

Today many states and counties have put their records online, so it is much easier if you can just pull up the records online. In addition, there are many free and subscription websites dedicated to providing databases for many of the above records.

A few of the subscription sites are:

- Ancestry.com
- Archives.com
- FindMyPast.com
- Genealogy.com
- MyTrees.com

Some of the free genealogy database websites are:

- Access Genealogy
- FamilySearch
- FindAGrave
- FreeUKGenealogy
- HeritageQuest Online
- Olive Tree Genealogy
- RootsWeb
- USGenWeb
- WorldGenWeb

DNA Search

Many people come to a roadblock in researching their family history. This is because they can't find the records or the records don't exist. That's where DNA comes in handy.

DNA is the molecule that encodes the genetic instructions for building and operating all living things and when you share a certain amount of DNA with someone, you are related to them. The amount of DNA you share with someone determines how closely you are related to them.

> **All humans share approximately 99.9% of their DNA with each other so the differences can be found in the remaining 0.1%** (National Human genome Research Institute 2018)!

DNA tests allow you to identify people you are related to and the approximate degree of that relationship. These tests also provide you with an estimate of your ethnic and geographic background. Once you have identified people you share DNA with, you can use information you find out about them to help map out your own family history.

Some are the major DNA testing sites are:

- 23andMe
- Ancestry DNA
- Family Tree DNA
- National Geographic Geno 2.0

A table comparing the above companies is provided in appendix J.

Tracing your family history is a massive undertaking, and how much of it you cover during your family reunion will depend on if someone in your family is already performing this research.

Some of the information you may want to cover if you include family history as one of your reunion activities includes:

- Family genealogy chart
- Brief history covering some key family members and/or ancestors
- DNA results for family members who have taking the test
- Family history games (family trivia game, etc.)

Whatever family history activity you decide to include, make sure you don't bit off more than you can chew, as you can go down a rabbit hole if you are not careful. If you are not very comfortable with it, remember *KISS* (keep it simple stupid!☺).

Free Time

You can easily get caught up in family time during a family reunion but for an extended family reunion, it's very important to leave time in the schedule for members to do whatever they want to do. I made the mistake in some of my earlier reunions by packing the schedule like sardines. What ended up happening in many cases was that people were showing up late for planned activities or not showing up at all! In their defense, why have reunions in interesting places if you don't have the opportunity to enjoy them?

So make sure you carve out a little bit of time every day during your reunion for people to venture out on their own. Also, if possible, be open to rescheduling group activities if they conflict with some newly discovered activity!

Icebreakers

It's always nice to kick off a family reunion with an icebreaker activity. Some relatives may not know each other that well or maybe you haven't seen a particular relative for ages. To get everybody reacquainted, icebreakers can be the best medicine.

Some of the categories of icebreakers are:

- Icebreaker games to get to know each other
- Icebreaker games to kick off meetings
- Icebreaker games to support team building
- Icebreaker games to improve teamwork and collaboration
- Just plain fun icebreaker games!

All of the above types of icebreakers can apply for a family reunion.

The list of potential icebreakers is longggggggg, so I won't attempt to provide examples. Just "google" icebreakers and you will find a lot of options.

Games

Just like icebreakers, the list of potential games to play during a family reunion is vast. Some of the types of games to consider though, are as follows:

- Adult-specific

- Board
- Children-specific
- Indoor
- Large group
- Outdoor
- Small group
- Social distancing
- Team building
- Theme-related

What I started doing after I had a few family reunions under my belt was to send out a survey to family members asking for suggestions on what games to play (among other things) during our next reunion. I received some really good feedback from these surveys, including games I would not have thought of or didn't even know existed.

Don't overdo it though when planning games. Remember that free time?

My family is competitive so I always provide awards to game winners. It's also fun to have award ceremonies!

A sample list of awards I have used in the past for game winners (and other awards) is provided in appendix K.

Movie Night
Many will say they don't go on vacation to watch television (many do though), but it can be fun to have a family movie night during your reunion. It could come after some other activity such as a family potluck meal, barbeque, or games, or it can stand on its own. I am not talking about going to a public movie theater to watch a movie. I am referring to having the whole clan watch a movie at your reunion location.

Some sites make it easy on you by having an on-site movie theater. This may come in the form of an indoor formal movie theater or a portable/semi-portable outdoor theater whereby a projector is used to project the movie image on a large surface (portable screen, side of a wall, etc.). Either way, you have it made. Pick your movie/night and bring the popcorn (if they don't provide it.)!

If you are not lucky enough to have your reunion at a site with a movie theater (or they aren't showing anything your family wants to watch), you can watch a movie in one of your units. But if you don't have enough room in your unit or the television is not big enough to experience the full impact, you can bring your movie theater with you! To pull this off, you will need the following equipment (at a minimum):

- Laptop, iPad, or another device capable of playing movies
- External portable speakers
- Portable projector
- Portable projector screen, blank wall, white sheet, or another place to display the movie
- Movie (from DVD, stored on computer, or from streaming service)
- Power/electricity
- Drinks and snacks

Laptop: Everybody brings some type of computer on vacation with them, right? If not, make sure you have your device is capable of playing movies. Also, you will need the appropriate cables to connect your computer to your projector unless you are able to connect wirelessly. It is best to have a laptop versus an iPad or other device as the laptop has better connectivity to the auxiliary devices (projector, external speakers, etc.).

Portable projector: Portable projectors aren't very expensive (can be less than $100) and they are light enough to fit in your carry-on luggage. They can weigh less than three pounds and project a screen size of over 170" (diagonal length). You can even use your iPad and smartphone to connect to many projectors instead of using a laptop.

Portable projector screen: A large light-colored blank wall makes a good surface to project movies on if you know you will have one. Curtains and sheets can also be used with good results if they are straight enough.

But there are also portable projector screens that can be used. These screens come in many sizes/weights and with/without stands. There are even some that are designed to be used outdoors. Prices can be as low as $25 on up to over $200, but you can get a good one with a stand in the $50 to $90 range. Some of these can also be broken down, put in their provided bag and loaded in carry-on luggage, and some are inflatable with a very small footprint when not inflated.

Movie: When selecting a movie, keep in mind it will need to appeal to most of the people in your party. You may want to have one movie night for children and another one for the adults.

Power/electricity: Don't forget to account for your power needs when planning your movie night. It's possible to get by with all battery-powered equipment but you may find that you will need access to electric outlets. Plan accordingly.

Drinks and snacks: Popcorn, anyone? You can't have a movie night without something to eat and drink. You are probably familiar with all the usual movie theater food and drink suspects from your movie-going days, including:

- Popcorn
- Soda/soft drink/alcoholic drink
- Chips/nachos/fries
- Candies
- Ice cream
- Milkshake
- Fried chicken/chicken nuggets

Select from these and other options that fit with your reunion members.

Seminars/Workshops

A smart idea we have at some of our family reunions is to have seminars or talks on different subjects of interest. If you have family members with expertise on particular subjects, why not have them volunteer to give talks on their subject. These can be topics related to their profession or something they research.

Suggested guidelines for your presentations are:

- Goal is to provide useful information that someone in the family can use to enhance the quality of their life
- Presentations can be in any form
- If you are going to give a PowerPoint presentation (recommended):
    - First page should be the title page with name of seminar, author, and date
    - Email your presentation to me or provide a CD so I can project the presentation on a projector
    - Plan on taking between 15 and 30 minutes for your presentation
- Provide handouts, if appropriate
    - Note that I will be emailing all the PowerPoint presentations to everyone after the reunion
- These will be informal presentations. Anyone with knowledge of the subject should feel free to communicate that knowledge
- Ask for questions at the end
- Topics to cover:
    - Define the subject
    - Why it is important

- Supporting data
- Benefits/issues
- Guidelines
- Personal experiences
- Recommendations
- References
  - Where to find additional information

Picnics

I discussed picnics in the food section of this book, so I won't go into too much detail here, but keep in mind that picnics aren't just for eating! They are a tried and true family reunion stable and if you have the opportunity to have one, you will have a blast.

The key to a good picnic is to make sure it is clear who will bring what and to schedule it early enough that people have to starve before the food is ready. Also, assign the dish that takes the longest to cook (ribs anyone?) to someone who has both the skill and the reliability to get started early so everyone's not waiting on them to finish.

Bon appétit, everyone!

Reunion Remembrance Book

Reunion remembrance books can be a great keepsake to reminisce about your event after it's gone. I talked about cookbooks earlier and the process of generating those. The process is similar with remembrance books, except the contents are different. You will be focusing on the key events from your reunion in the remembrance book and making them come alive with pictures and describing the most memorial moments, feelings, and comradery.

Since you will be adding pictures, you may need to secure releases from people who can be identified in the pictures to protect yourself legally, especially if you plan on publishing the book and making it available for purchase by a larger audience.

Remembrance books have come a long way from the old scrapbooking days. Today's books are generally of a higher quality while not necessarily being more expensive than the old scrapbooks. The elements you will want to include in your book are:

- Family name page: The primary family surname.
- Reunion summary: Date(s), location, theme, and other key reunion data.
- Attendee list: List of everyone who attended the event (including contact information). You may also want to include a family tree to show how everyone is connected (including distant relatives).

- Photo galleries: Photos providing a good summary of the event, including labels to make it easier to determine what was going on and who was doing what to whom.
- Reunion events: You can combine with the photo gallery or keep them separate and maybe have one or two pictures of each event in this section.
- Reunion recipes: If you are not doing a family cookbook, you can add some of the key recipes used during the reunion here.

Don't forget to identify the person or persons who will be creating your remembrance book prior to the event so they can make sure to keep copious notes during the event! This person will also need to coordinate with the family photographer (if you have one) to make sure they will have the pictures they will need.

Shopping

Shopping can also be a fun activity for some family members. These can be both planned and ad hoc shopping trips. This can also be an activity that individual family members can partake of during their free time. Some of the types of shopping establishments to consider are:

- Shopping malls
- Outlet malls
- Local jewelry stores
- Local art stores
- Farmers markets
- Flea markets
- Other specialty stores

Don't shop 'til you drop though, or you will miss out on all the other reunion activities!

Sunday Worship Service

Sunday worship services may be one activity your group is interested in. If so, you will want to research churches at your destination to find one that fits your needs (denomination, location, dress code, indoor/outdoor, and so on). This can be a way to give thanks for your blessings and for the opportunity to vacation and fellowship with family.

If you aren't into a formal religious situation but you want to commune in some spiritual way, you can also go to a place that allows you to appreciate each other in a peaceful, relaxing, tranquil, or serene environment.

You could also do something like a Sunday picnic or other family gathering.

However you would want to shape it, sometimes it's good to schedule an activity that allows you to celebrate the love you have for life and your extended family.

Talent Show

America's got talent, what about your family? Performing a talent show can be a fun activity during a family reunion. It's a good bonding activity and you may find out that participants have talents you didn't know they had!

To pull your show off and to increase your chances of success, you should roughly follow the following steps:

- Call for talent: At least six months prior to your reunion, you need to communicate to all reunion participants that a talent show will be one of the activities and that anyone who wanted to show off one of their talents should let you know, including what their talent is and any equipment/resources they would need to perform their talent. Follow up with people once per month to make sure they are on track to be ready to perform during the reunion.
- Preliminary program/schedule: About one month prior to the event, send out the official draft talent show program schedule. This schedule will list all the participants, the name of their talent, and the order in which they will perform. Make sure they know this is a preliminary schedule that could change.

  Having a schedule makes everything real and gets people excited to showcase their own talent as well as to witness the talents of their family members. It also serves as a reminder for people to step up their preparation if they are a little behind schedule in preparing for their performance.

- Judging: The people you select to judge the talents can't themselves be in the talent show of course but how do you select an impartial set of judges? Some options for judge selection includes:
  - Find someone at your reunion site who may be willing to serve as a judge.
  - Use family members but have them recuse themselves from judging their immediate family members.

  You should also communicate the criteria the judges are using to rate the talents (having criteria also makes it easier for the judges to rate the performances). Some criteria to consider include:
  - Audience response
  - Creativity

- Originality
- Quality
- Stage appearance

A sample card that can be used to rate participants is:

Talent Show Judging Criteria			
Contestant Name:			
Criteria	Fair (10 points): Olay effort but nothing to write	Good (20 points): Surprisingly good with a few minor	Excellent (30 points): Outstanding, I can't believe they did that!
Audience Response			
Creativity			
Originality			
Quality			
Stage Appearance			
Total Points:			
Grand Total Points:			

- The stage: You will need to set up an area that can be used as a stage for people to perform their talent. This can be a conference room, the living room of your unit, or an outdoor space conducive to executing a talent show.
- Awards: You can't have a talent show without awards, so at a minimum you need to have award certificates to present to the winners. You may also want to present prizes to the lucky winners.

Tours

Formal guided group tours are another optional family reunion activity. These allow you to experience something new at your reunion locale without having to worry about coordinating transportation or finding your way around. These tours can either be in your immediate area or constitute day trips to areas within a few hours of your location.

Types of tours include:

- Adventure
- Culinary, food & wine
- Cultural
- Ecological
- Religious
- Sea excursion
- Shore excursion

- Sightseeing
- Sporting (cycle, rock climbing, etc.)
- Whale watching

You may want to reserve your tours ahead of time to ensure your desired time slot is available, but sometimes you can find price discounts once you arrive at your destination.

Nightlife

If you want to "get your groove on" during your family reunion and there wasn't enough heat during the day to get it done, nightlife is what you want! This is one activity that generally won't include everyone at your reunion, especially if children are attending your reunion but you will want to provide some options for those who would like to partake. Of course there are some nighttime events that include children, such as the fireworks on Hilton Head Island every Tuesday night in the summer.

During the planning for your reunion, look for highly rated nightlife for your location. As with some other activities, you can check TripAdvisor or google "nightlife" for your destination.

Those in your party who do plan on enjoying the nightlife should join forces and go as a group. Don't forget to have a designated driver or two if the group will be driving to their destination. Another option is to take public transportation (cab, Uber, private shuttle, etc.) so you don't have to worry about drinking and driving.

Final Night Dinner/Banquet/Award Presentations

It's always nice to cap off your family reunion with a final night dinner. This "Last Supper" allows you to have a formal close to your event and to reminisce on all the fun you had during the week. I also use this time to present awards to winners of all the events we held during the week.

This also may be the last opportunity you have to stay goodbye to participants as people normally would be leaving at different times the following morning. Make sure to get any contact or other information you still need during this time.

Final Morning Farewell

If you do have time during the departure day, you can schedule a departure day farewell to say our final goodbyes. This often takes the form of a final day group breakfast.

If the whole group can't make it, you may want to leave it on the schedule for those who are able to participate.

Let's Rate It

After all the fun is over, it's worthwhile to solicit feedback from the participants to determine:

- ➢ What did they like?
- ➢ What didn't they like?
- ➢ Suggestions for improvement?

This can be an informal activity you perform on the final night or you can pass out a survey to solicit formal responses to be returned to you at a later date.

Contingency Planning

> "The plans of the diligent lead to profit as surely as haste leads to poverty" (Bible, New International Version 2011, Proverbs 21:5).

Murphy's Law states that "things that can go wrong will go wrong" (Wikipedia, the free encyclopedia n.d.). If you believe the veracity of this old saying, then you will want to make contingency plans to offset the impacts of things going wrong during your family reunion.

The mantra of most contingency planning aficionados is to focus on the risks that are most likely to happen and those that have the most negative impact if they were to happen. This should be your focus when deciding which contingencies to plan for. For family reunions, these risks include flight cancelations, people getting sick, lost passports, and so on.

To address potential risks associated with your family reunion, you may want to make contingency plans that cover some of the following items.

Emergency Response Plan

An emergency response plan can provide clear direction on what participants should do in case of certain types of emergencies that may occur during your reunion. It documents the responsibilities, actions, and required information for reacting to emergency events. Items you may want to address in your plan include:

- Identify possible emergencies and a plan to mitigate them
    - Behavior issues
    - Civil unrest or other security-related issues
    - Cell phone failure in remote areas
    - Injury, illness or death of participants
    - Lost passport and/or visa
    - Pandemics
    - Theft or other crimes
    - Vehicle accidents and breakdowns
    - Weather-related emergencies
- Contacts – official and personal
- Risk assessment: access the US State Department for information on any potential risks in the area of your reunion

It can be very frustrating when you need to call someone and you don't have their contact information. That's why you should include an emergency contact list as part of your emergency response plan. Some local contacts to include are:

- Cell phone numbers for all reunion participants
- Hospitals
- Ambulance
- Police
- Fire department
- Health insurance contacts
- US embassy (for international travel)
- Emergency contact information for someone not attending the reunion

COVID-19

COVID-19 presents a new issue for travel contingency planners. Given the expert opinion that COVID-19 may be an ongoing concern, you will need to address it in your reunion contingency planning.

The first step is to ensure that all reunion participants have their updated COVID-19 vaccination if possible. If a participant is able to get the vaccine but chooses not to for some reason, you will need to plan on how to address that issue. If a negative COVID-19 test is required to enter your reunion destination or to return to your home country, make sure you provide information to participants on where they can receive the test and the specific guidelines to follow for the impacted country or locale.

If being fully vaccinated is a requirement to travel, make sure all vaccinated participants have a copy of their vaccination card or other required documentation. It's a good idea to take a picture of your vaccination card with your cell phone so you have a digital record.

Review the COVID-19 entrance/exit requirements for all relevant countries and states, as well as the requirements/guidelines for all the facilities you will be visiting during your reunion.

Whether you are vaccinated or not, it's very important that everyone follows the COVID-19 preventive measures required by appropriate authorities such as wearing masks and staying the defined number of feet apart.

If someone in your group does get COVID-19, know what the current isolation requirements, isolate that person and you may want to arrange for all other reunion participants to get a COVID-19 test to ensure it has not been spread.

If a participant tests positive and can't return back to their home country, have plans in place for that person or persons to have a place to stay until they test negative or they satisfy any other requirement to return home.

Travel Insurance

We all hope that bad things don't happen during our family reunions but sometimes our hopes are in vain as sometimes people get sick, have accidents, reservations get canceled, and so on. If any of these things happen, travel insurance can be your friend.

There are many types of travel insurance, including:

- Accidental death
- Emergency medical assistance
- Flight cancelation
- Lost/damaged luggage
- Medical evacuation
- Trip cancelation and interruption

If you have any preexisting conditions, you may want to make sure that they are covered by your insurance.

You may find that your private medical insurance covers you during your family reunion for medical-related costs. That is normally the case if you are vacationing in your home country, but often that's not the case if you are traveling internationally. Even if you are covered by your personal insurance, if your coverage is "out of network" it may be cheaper to purchase travel insurance.

You can go directly to an insurance provider's website to purchase travel insurance, but sometimes it's better to check out an insurance provider comparison website to find a plan that best fits you. Some of the better insurance comparison sites are:

- AARDY – https://www.aardy.com/
- Allianz – https://www.allianztravelinsurance.com/
- G1G – https://www.g1g.com/
- Insure My Trip – https://www.insuremytrip.com/
- Square Mouth – https://www.squaremouth.com
- Travelex – https://www.travelexinsurance.com/
- Travel Guard – https://www.travelguard.com/

Also, you may find that you have some level of travel insurance coverage through your credit card or your home/car insurance policy.

Planning For the Next One

Now that the event is over, it's time to sit back and think about the next one!

Lessons Learned
Before you can do that though, you need to document lessons learned from the last one:

- How well did things go?
- What could be done better?
- Suggestions for the next one

To address the above questions, you need to hear "straight from the horse's mouth" by surveying the reunion participants. Informal feedback should be documented during the reunion with a semiformal feedback session on the last day of the event. But it is very important to follow up with formal detailed feedback by way of a formal survey. You will be able to get valuable feedback with a survey and when participants know you are taking their opinions into account, they will be more willing to attend the next one as well as to pass on positive feedback to those who did not attend the event.

You and your reunion planning committee should also perform your own lessons learned assessment to improve on the next event. You may have noticed a number of things during the event. Make sure you have a "Lessons Learned" form/document so you can easily add notes on these items as they occur.

Gathering More Feedback
Doing a survey helps you to gain insight into how to solve issues you had to deal with during the most recent event, such as problems getting people to pay their dues or being on time for activities.

Some questions/feedback you can include in the survey are:

- What time of year would you prefer to have the next reunion?
- How much time are you willing to contribute toward supporting the next reunion?
- Are you interested in joining the family reunion planning committee?
- How much money are you willing to contribute to make the next reunion successful?
- Where would you like the next event to be held (country, state, city)?
- What type of lodging would you like to have?
- How many days do you think the ideal reunion should be?
- How far are you willing to travel?

- How many people in your immediate family do you think would be interested in attending the next event?
- What type of activities would you like to have at the next event?
- Do you have any theme ideas?
- List the top 5 things you liked about the previous reunion?
- List the top 5 things you didn't like about the previous reunion?
- What did you think of the reunion overall?
- What could we have done differently/better?
- What did you think about the decorations?
- How often would you like to have family reunions?

Putting It All Together

Once you have done your lessons learned and solicited additional feedback from people, you will want to use that information to develop a *strawman* planning document for the next reunion. A family reunion strawman document is a brainstormed draft detail document that forms the basis for your next reunion planning. It addresses all the issues identified from your lessons learned and participant survey and updates your previous reunion planning document. This is a living document that gets updated and matured as your reunion planning progresses.

Once your strawman is complete, you may want to send it out to all potential reunion participants to get additional feedback from them before you start putting too much meat into your planning.

Document Publication & Distribution

If you were planning on providing any final documents to reunion participants such as cookbooks, reunion keepsake books, and so on, you will need to complete these tasks after the reunion. You will want to provide this data in as timely a manner as possible while the memories are still hot.

During the reunion, give the participants a realistic estimate of when you will be able to provide the above publications and solicit assistance as necessary to get it done. If the schedule changes, it would be nice to notify folks to keep them informed.

If there is a cost to provide these documents, make sure you communicate any payment members will need to make in order to receive the documents (including shipping costs, if applicable). If items will be available for purchase on a website (Amazon, Barnes & Noble, etc.), provide the web address where the item can be purchased.

SECTION 2: Sample Reunion Itinerary

☞ Section Highlights

- Overview
- Table A – People Locations & Game Information
- Table B – Planned Activities

The Family Reunion Bible

Overview

I have provided a lot of information that could be overwhelming if you haven't planned an extended family reunion before. To help you out, this section provides a sample day-by-day itinerary to give you an idea of how to plan a 7-day family reunion. I use a Microsoft Excel spreadsheet to generate my itineraries but you can use any other software that works for you.

I generally like to include where family members are staying as part of my itinerary to make it convenient. Ideally, everyone is in the same resort but this is not always possible, so you want to list each resort/accommodation and the people in each unit.

If we are playing games, I also provide details on the games as part of the itinerary. I provide some information on how the games will be played and list each of the games with comments if necessary.

The below tables provide a sample itinerary.

Table A provides the following:

- People locations:
- Resort name:
- Phone:
- Unit type:
- List of people:
- # Game players:
- Total people:
- # Packages:
- Activities:
- Contests:
- Bonus:
- General notes:

Table B provides the following information:

- Date:
- Day:
- Activity:
- Location:
- Other activities:

You may notice that there is a lot of open space in the table B itinerary. That is on purpose. You want to leave a fair amount of open time where family members can selectively do their own thing. If you fill up too much time with mandatory planned events, you will find that people will begin to show up late or not at all.

If you are having your family reunion in an interesting vacation spot, you want to be able to fully enjoy where you are. This extra time can be periods where you can do things individually or with a subset of family members.

The sample itinerary in table B lists the mandatory activities and the sample Vacation Reference charts in appendix L provide an expanded list of activities that individual family members can partake of at their discretion. So you can pick and choose the non-mandatory activities you are interested in taking part in. Remember, it's all about what you and the family want to do!

Table A – People Locations & Game Information

	People Locations					
Resort Name:	HGVC Tuscany Village	HGVC Tuscany Village	Grand Beach	Grand Beach	Marriott's Grande Vista	
Phone:						
Unit Type:	3 Bed	2 Bed	3 Bed	2 Bed	2 Bed	
Sleeps	8	6	8	6	8	
List of People:						Grand Total
# Game Players:						
Total People						
# Packages:						
Activities:						

Contests: Various contests will be held through out the week. Points will be won for each contest. The person having the most points at the end of the week will win a 7 day timeshare vacation from a list of available units and locations! (accomodations only)

	Contest	Comments
1	Wii bowling	
2	Name Search	Points for each game won
3	Family Feud	
4	Cards	
5	Game Show	

Table B – Planned Activities

Planned Activities

Date	Day	Activity	Location
23-Jun	FRI		
23-Jun	FRI	Check into resort	
23-Jun	FRI		
23-Jun	FRI		
23-Jun	FRI		
24-Jun	SAT		
24-Jun	SAT		
24-Jun	SAT		
24-Jun	SAT	Official start of reunion	
24-Jun	SAT		
24-Jun	SAT	Informal get to together	
24-Jun	SAT	(Pass out Sunday activities only)	
24-Jun	SAT		
25-Jun	SUN		
25-Jun	SUN		
25-Jun	SUN	Church Service	
25-Jun	SUN		
25-Jun	SUN		
25-Jun	SUN	Orientation	Henry's Unit
25-Jun	SUN	Family History Briefing: Ancestry Basics	Henry's Unit
25-Jun	SUN	Video of last year's reunion	Henry's Unit
25-Jun	SUN		
25-Jun	SUN		
25-Jun	SUN		
26-Jun	MON		
26-Jun	MON		
26-Jun	MON	Family History Briefing: DNA Basics	
26-Jun	MON	Wii bowling game	Henry's Unit
26-Jun	MON		
26-Jun	MON		
26-Jun	MON		

Table B (Continued)

Planned Activities

Date	Day	Activity	Location
27-Jun	TUE		
27-Jun	TUE		
27-Jun	TUE		
27-Jun	TUE	Family History Briefing: Haplogroups, Human Origins	
27-Jun	TUE		
27-Jun	TUE	Family Feud Game	Henry's Unit
27-Jun	TUE		
27-Jun	TUE	Family Members Name Search Game	Henry's Unit
27-Jun	TUE		
27-Jun	TUE	Pot Luck Dinner	Henry's Unit
27-Jun	TUE		
28-Jun	WED		
28-Jun	WED		
28-Jun	WED	Men's Get Together	
28-Jun	WED		
28-Jun	WED	Family History Briefing: Health Reports, Racial Mixture	
28-Jun	WED	Card game	Henry's Unit
28-Jun	WED		
29-Jun	THU		
29-Jun	THU		
29-Jun	THU		
29-Jun	THU	Bonus jar guess due	
29-Jun	THU		
29-Jun	THU		
29-Jun	THU	Family History Briefing: Our Ancestors, DNA Relatives	
29-Jun	THU		
29-Jun	THU	Game Show contest	Henry's Unit
29-Jun	THU		

Table B (Continued)

Planned Activities

Date	Day	Activity	Location
30-Jun	FRI		
30-Jun	FRI		
30-Jun	FRI		
30-Jun	FRI	Farewell Dinner	
30-Jun	FRI		
30-Jun	FRI	Video of this	Henry's Unit
30-Jun	FRI	Winner notification	Henry's Unit
30-Jun	FRI	Discussions for 2019 reunion	Henry's Unit
30-Jun	FRI		
30-Jun	FRI		
1-Jul	SAT	Check out	
1-Jul	SAT	Farewell breakfast (TBD)	
1-Jul	SAT		
1-Jul	SAT		

SECTION 3: Templates and Worksheets

☞ Section Highlights

- ➢ Budget Worksheet
- ➢ Contact List
- ➢ Reunion Survey

The Family Reunion Bible

Budget Worksheet

Example of Items to Budget (Continued)				
Estimated Turnout:				
Estimated # people contributing money:				
Estimated contribution per contributor:				
Budget Item	Unit Cost	Per Item	Total Items	Estimated Cost
Communications				$ -
envelopes				$ -
long distance phone charges (don't forget faxes)!				$ -
printer paper				$ -
printer ink (black, cyan, blue, and magenta)				$ -
Stamps				$ -
				$ -
Equipment Rental or Purchase				$ -
tables				$ -
chairs				$ -
shelters				$ -
grills				$ -
pa system				$ -
music equipment				$ -
photo or video equipment				$ -
game equipment (volleyball net, balls, cards, etc)				$ -
Fees				$ -
park or camping reservation fees				$ -
				$ -
Decorations				
Food				$ -
groceries (food and drink)				$ -
paper plates				$ -
cups				$ -
plastic silverware				$ -
disposable table cloths				$ -
charcoal briquets				$ -
restaurants				$ -
caterers				$ -
banquet room rental				$ -
taxes				$ -
tips and gratuities				$ -

Example of Items to Budget (Continued)

	Estimated Turnout:			
	Estimated # people contributing money:			
	Estimated contribution per contributor:			

Budget Item	Unit Cost	Per Item	Total Items	Estimated Cost
Printing				$ -
invitations				$ -
reminder mailers				$ -
Welcome packet/handouts				$ -
Welcome banner				$ -
Registration guest book				$ -
surveys				$ -
evaluation forms				$ -
name tags				$ -
printing software				$ -
t-shirts				$ -
newsletters				$ -
family directory				$ -
certificates				$ -
family tree wall chart				$ -
family cookbook				$ -
				$ -
Services				$ -
professional photograpy or videography				$ -
reunion planners (if you chicken out doing it yourself)				$ -
entertainers (magicians, band, clowns, etc)				$ -
				$ -
Supplies				$ -
film				$ -
blank video tapes				$ -
decorations				$ -
prizes or awards				$ -
DVDs				$ -
				$ -
Prizes				$ -
Timeshare Grand prize				$ -
				$ -
				$ -
				$ -
				$ -

Total Costs: $ -

Contact List

Name	Family Vacation Atendee Contact List				Telephone Number	Email Address
	Home Address				Telephone Number	Email Address
	Street	City	State	Zip		

Reunion Survey

Sample Reunion Survey				
Survey Question	**Response (Circle or enter information)**			
Time of Year	Spring	Summer	Fall	Winter
Time can you contribute	None	A little	few days/mo.	Lots
Money can you contribute	Zero	$25	$50	$100 or more
Recommended reunion location	1st choice	2nd choice	3rd choice	4th choice
Recommended lodging	Camping	Hotel	Resort	Other
Recommended length of reunion	1 day	3 days	1 week	Other
How far to travel	3 hour drive	6 hour drive	6 hour flight	Other
Attending family members	1	2	4	Other
Recommended activities	Option 1	Option 2	Option 3	Option 4
Theme ideas	Option 1	Option 2	Option 3	Option 4
Top things you liked	Option 1	Option 2	Option 3	Option 4
Top things you didn't like	Option 1	Option 2	Option 3	Option 4
Frequency of reunions	Twice per year	Once per year	Bi-annually	Other
rientation feedback	Bad	Good	Excellent	Other
Gift bags feedback	Bad	Good	Excellent	Other
Games feedback	Bad	Good	Excellent	Other
Attractions feedback	Bad	Good	Excellent	Other
Food feedback	Bad	Good	Excellent	Other
Shopping feedback	Bad	Good	Excellent	Other
Entertainment feedback	Bad	Good	Excellent	Other
Church feedback	Bad	Good	Excellent	Other
Prizes feedback	Bad	Good	Excellent	Other
What did you think about the reunion				
What could be done better				
How did you like the decorations				
Miscellaneous feedback				

APPENDIX A: Puerto Vallarta Newsletter

The Family Reunion Bible

Appendix A

Thomas Family Winter Newsletter

Thomas Family Publishing

Thomas Family Vacation

Hello Thomas Family!

The purpose of this newsletter is to provide you with a heads up on our next.

As you are aware, we submitted a survey September 2017 soliciting feedback on all aspects of our last family vacation. The survey also provided a list of destinations for a future family vacation. Three locations tied for first place: Cancun Mexico, New Orleans Louisiana, and Tampa Florida. Since we have never had a family vacation outside the United States, we decided Mexico would be a good spot. Some family members are already scheduled to go to Cancun in 2018 though so we decided on Puerto Vallarta Mexico instead.

Puerto Vallarta & Cancun are very similar as far as beaches, nightlife, activities, etc.

Puerto Vallarta is a resort town on Mexico's Pacific coast, in Jalisco state. It is known for its beaches, water sports and nightlife scene. Its cobblestone center is home to the ornate Nuestra Señora de Guadalupe church, boutique shops and a range of restaurants and bars. El Malecón is a beachside promenade with contemporary sculptures, as well as bars, lounges and nightclubs.

This Mexican paradise offers visitors a dozen sandy, sun-kissed beaches, plenty of colorful festivals and celebrations, tropical jungles to explore and many a mountainside to traverse. Therefore, let's go to Puerto Vallarta!

Puerto Vallarta Malecon

Volume 1, Issue 1
December 2017

Special points of interest:

- Family Vacation
- Vidanta Resorts
- Puerto Vallarta
- Nuevo Vallarta
- Beaches
- History
- Culture

Inside this issue:

Headquarters	1
Resort lineup	2
Resort Details	2
The Park	3
Lodging	3
Transportation	3
Funding	4

Thomas Family Vacation Headquarters

Our next family vacation will be headquartered at the Vidanta resorts in Nuevo Vallarta. This complex consists of 5 different resorts all sharing facilities on one large beachfront plot of land.

Nuevo Vallarta is a planned resort on Mexico's Pacific coast, just north of Puerto Vallarta. It sits on Banderas Bay, and is known for its golf courses, marina and long, sandy Nuevo Vallarta beach. A short distance off the coast, the biodiverse Marieta Islands are home to wildlife, including dolphins, turtles and humpback whales. Nuevo Vallarta is one of the fastest growing beach destinations of Mexico and has the second-highest number of hotels in the country.

Vidanta Nuevo Vallarta Resort Lineup

There are five resorts on the Vidanta property in Nuevo Vallarta:

1. Sea Garden: A fun, comfortable resort hotel with some of the best service in Mexico
2. Mayan Palace: A favorite with families everywhere featuring fresh, spacious accommodations
3. The Grand Mayan: A haven of modern comfort and high-end relaxation for the whole family
4. The Grand Bliss: This modern take on luxury offers a stylish and sophisticated place to vacation
5. Grande Luxxe: The most exclusive of Vidanta's resorts and recipient of the AAA 5 Diamond Award.

Vidanta has cultivated a collection of resorts where families from all over the world can come to spend time exploring, relaxing, and making memories together. Vidanta Nuevo Vallarta offers the ultimate resort vacation. It has been designed to provide a high-end experience full of options: 40 plus restaurants and lounges to try, three golf courses and a golf academy, a shopping plaza, two indulgent spas, beautiful beaches, and countless pools. It has everything you could want in a resort.

Vidanta Nuevo Vallarta Site Map

Vidanta Nuevo Vallarta Resort At A Glance

This resort complex has much to offer including the following:

- Dining: Resort boasts over 25 restaurants, a Mercado Gourmet, and the street food of Mercado Mexico
- Entertainment: Take in amazing performances at Santuario, enjoy specialty theme nights, or check out nightly live music
- Pools: Tour the many pools, Aqua Park, Lazy River, and Mayan Water Slide
- Golf: Sharpen your game at either of the two designer courses or the famous Vidanta Golf Academies
- Spa: Find complete relaxation and renewal at either of the luxurious spas.

The World's Most Extraordinary Beach Resorts! Experience Happiness at Vidanta.

Brio or Spatium

Vidanta Nuevo Vallarta Resort At A Glance (Continued)

- Activities: Spend your vacation learning, exploring, adventuring, and having fun with their many activities, including options for kids, adults, and the whole family
- Shopping: At the center of Vidanta Nuevo Vallarta's shopping experience is La Plaza, a three-story facility fitted with specialty boutiques, food counters, a bazaar, and so much more
- Over 1 mile of beachfront
- Wooden pathways throughout the resort
- 2500 acres of paradise
- The Grand Vidanta Convention Center
- Almaverde: 40-acre farm which yields over 65 types of fruits and vegetables that are used throughout the resort!

Vidanta Nuevo Vallarta

Appendix A

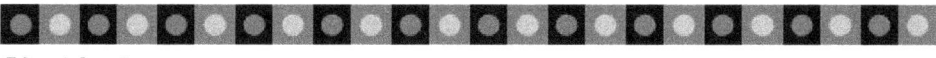

The Parks

In 2019 Vidanta will debut The Parks, a culture-shifting new approach to theme parks. This new concept in family vacationing will fuse luxury with imagination, creating a fantastical world where adventures leap to life through immersive rides, attractions, and interactive performances. Neighboring The Parks will be high-end new resort hotels where guests can continue to experience the fantastic, even when they've left the theme park for the day!

The Parks will allow visitors from all over to experience a series of immersive wonderlands. It starts with never-before-seen attractions and groundbreaking experiential adventures, all planned, designed, and executed by the most accomplished and revered experts in the field.

The Parks will offer guests a variety of extraordinary experiences that extend well beyond the attractions. They will feature a variety of imaginative and delicious dining options, including carts, markets, restaurants, and cafeterias, all of which will showcase Vidanta's gourmet every day approach to food.

The Parks are slated to be open in mid-2019 so it could be open during our Thomas Family Vacation.

Vidanta Nuevo Vallarta Theme Parks

Lodging

Lodging has always been a challenge for our Thomas Family Vacations. That will be especially true for the next one. In order for the planning committee to secure lodging for people you would need send payment by May 1, 2018. After that date the committee organizers will have limited ability to secure lodging for others. A list of options though will be provided for people needing to secure their own accommodations. If you decide to secure your lodging through our planning committee the expected prices are as follows:

Resort Name	Prices* (TBR)		
	2 Bedroom	3 Bedroom	Per Person
Sea Garden	$1,200	$1,500	$300
Mayan Palace	$1,200	$1,500	$300
Grand Mayan	$1,300	$1,600	$350
Grand Bliss	$1,400	$1,700	$350
Grand Luxxe	$1,500	$1,800	$400

*Prices are subject to change. Keep in

"Our family is a circle of strength; founded on faith, joined in love, kept by God, together forever." -Unknown

mind that cheaper prices may be possible if you pay early!

Transportation

Since this will be a flying vacation for all of us, our transportation costs will be higher than normal. Thus, it is more important than ever for you to start saving for this expense. By putting aside a little every week, month, or pay period you can have this expense taken care of with minimum pain. The cost to fly to Puerto Vallarta will probably range from $400 to $700 depending on where you live. We are over 18 months away from the start of this vacation.

If you assume that the price will be $600 you would need to save around $35 a month per person. If you normally receive a tax return you could also use your 2018 tax refund to pay for your airfare tickets.

Make sure you consider all possible cities to fly out of to minimize your costs. You should also research all the discount airlines operating in your area including JetBlue, Southwest, Spirit, and Frontier.

Flying the friendly skies to Mexico!

Thomas Family Publishing

C/O Henry Thomas

www.emailaddress.com

We're on the Web!
example.com

Funding Vacation Expenses

There are a lot of expenses associated with pulling off our Thomas Family Vacations: Office supplies, certificates, prizes, tote bags, etc.

We need Money!

The planning committee can't continue to fund these costs without support from other participants. We understand that this family vacation will be more expensive for some because of the airfare cost and we will be looking at ways to reduce the cost of this vacation but we will still require funds to make this happen. Some ideas for covering the funding includes:

- Dues
- Auctions
- Raffle tickets
- Bake sale
- Craft sale
- Selling dinners
- Recycling
- Yard sales
- Family cookbook

Over the course of the next several months the planning committee will be evaluating these and other options to fund our next family vacation. If anyone has any additional ideas please pass them on the Thomas Family Vacation Planning Committee.

Remember, family reunions are an important part of family life. They can help preserve fond memories, favorite recipes, stories and, most importantly, relationships that will last for generations. Given a chance, family reunions and celebrations can provide family members with important values, strong and lasting bonds, and a deep sense of belonging that they can pass on to their children and their grandchildren.

Let's find a way to get this done!

APPENDIX B: Reunion Code of Conduct

Appendix B

Reunion Code of Conduct

Purpose

We are committed to providing a friendly, safe, and welcoming environment for all reunion participants and people we interact with regardless of age, gender, sexual orientation, gender identity, gender expression, disability, ethnicity, race or religion.

This code of conduct outlines our expectations for participant behavior as well as the potential consequences for unacceptable behavior displayed during this reunion.

Please help us to realize a safe and positive reunion experience for everyone.

Scope

We expect all reunion participants to abide by this code of conduct at all times, at all reunion venues, and at all reunion-related events.

Host Lodging & Facilities

Participant agrees to maintain the reunion lodging and facilities in as good condition as it was at the start of the reunion except for ordinary wear and tear. The participant is expected to pay for all repairs, replacements and damages caused by the neglect of the participant or their dependents. Participant also agrees not to damage the property of others.

Participant agrees to abide by all other rules, terms and code of conduct applicable to the host location.

Expected Behavior

- Be considerate and respectful of all people and property during the reunion.
- Be mindful of your surroundings and of your fellow participants. Alert reunion planning team members if you notice a concerning situation and if you feel there is an emergency, contact the police or dial 911.

Page 1 of 2

_____
Initial

Unacceptable Behavior

- Intimidating, harassing, abusive, discriminatory, derogatory, or demeaning conduct
- Deliberate intimidation, stalking, photographing or recording an individual against their wishes, and disruption of talks or other events.

Consequences

We are family and we hope that we will not have to deal with unacceptable behavior from reunion participants. If this type of behavior is displayed, the guilty party will be asked to stop the unacceptable behavior.

If the participant refuses to stop the unacceptable behavior, we will take measures we deem appropriate to deal with the situation.

Drugs and Alcohol

All family members are expected to consume alcohol responsibly and at all times to respect property, reunion participants, and others.

Illegal drug use is not recommended.

Reporting

If you are the subject of unacceptable behavior, or notice that someone else is subject to unacceptable behavior, please notify reunion planning team members if you are not able to or not comfortable with neutralizing the situation yourself. If it is an emergency situation, please call the police or dial 911.

Health & Safety

If you witness any unsafe situation, please notify the appropriate person to have the issue taken care of.

_____   _____

Participant Signature   **Date**

APPENDIX C: Family Reunion Checklists

The Family Reunion Bible

Appendix C

Reunion Planning Checklist

\multicolumn{2}{c}{Reunion Planning Checklist}	
Prior to Reunion	**Activity/Action**
One Year to 18 Months	Decide that you want to have a reunion
	Discuss with a small set of potential participants
	Survey larger group to determine interest
	Select a planning committee and schedule meetings
	Assign responsibilities to committee members
	Research and select potential locations and dates
	Survey family members on locations and dates
	Select location and dates
	Draft budget
	Setup online information site (family website page, Facebook page, etc.)
	Select a theme
	Communicate location and dates to all
	Draft strawman schedule (food, activities, games, etc.)
12 Months	Secure lodging
	Once a month planning team meetings (plus adhoc meetings as required)
	Apply for licenses, permits, etc.
9 Months	Send updated newsletter to provide current status
	Order prizes, gifts, mementos, decorations, etc.
	Start generating reunion handouts
	Initiate fund-raising activities
	Research reunion ideas and activities
	Schedule events/activities requiring advance booking
	Start transportation search (airfare, train, bus, etc.)
6 Months	Send out dues reminder
	Twice a month planning team meetings (plus adhoc meetings as required)
	Follou-up with non-responders and other potential attendees
	Confirm reservations
	Status and update fund-raising activities

Reunion Planning Checklist (Continued)	
Prior to Reunion	**Activity/Action**
3 Months	Send out another update to participants
	Prepare and finalize handouts
	Order additional souvenirs, T-shirts, etc.
	Finalize schedule
1 Month	Finalize reunion package
	Once a week planning team meetings (plus adhoc meetings as required)
	Finalize responsibilities during the reunion
	Communicate key responsibilities, checklists, first day activities, etc. to participants
2 Weeks	Finalize list of participants
	Confirm all reunion details
	Print out reunion handouts
1 Week	Add any last minute attendees
	Check with attendees to address any concerns or questions
	Update budget
	Confirm any last minute details with committee members
Day Of	Check into lodging
	Check on all reservations/services
	Set-up and decoration reunion site
	Set up sign-in area with handouts, food, drinks, etc.
	Welcome family members as they arrive
	Schedule orientation
After	Send out survey to participants
	Lessons learned
	Gather additional feedback
	Draft planning for next reunion
	Generate, publish, and distribute planned documents to participants

Appendix C

Vacation Travel Checklist

Vacation Travel Checklist			
(Check: Y=Yes, N=No, N/A=Not Applicable)			
Category/Description	Ck	Category/Description	Ck
Before Leaving Home		**Cleaning Items**	
Arrange to have lawn mowed/watered		Bounce	
Arrange to have trash taken out		Carpet cleaner	
Arrange to have someone check house		Clothes hangers	
Notify police		Clothes pins to hang from shower rod	
Call resort to confirm exchange		Dishwasher soap	
Call resort with special requests		Fabric softener sheets/Fabreze	
Disconnect garage door openers		Large bar soap X 2	
Adjust thermostat to save energy		Laundry soap (All-in-1/3-1 product)	
Set email groups to "no email"		Liquid dish soap	
Set up lamp timers		Lysol Spray	
Shut off ice maker		Plastic laundry bags	
Stop mail and newspaper		Scrubber/brillo pad/SOS pad, sponge	
Tell neighbor you're leaving		Stain removal stick	
Turn down hot water heater		Trash bags (large and small)	
Turn off water to washing machine		Wet wipes	
Verify insurance coverages			
Set up auto houseplant water drippers		**Documents and Photocopies**	
Unplug home electronic equipment		Reservations for accommodations	
Leave emergency contact info		Auto rental confirmations	
Tuck a dryer sheet into each suitcase		Driver's License	
20-ounce soda bottle tops to replace pump and flip tops		Exchange Confirmation	
		Medical Insurance Forms	
Extras		Passports and Visas	
Entertainments or other local coupon books		RX's and eyeglass info	
Water bottle		Short Records	
Booster Seat for rental car		Personal auto insurance policy number	
		Airline tickets	
		Reservations for activities purchased/ reserved before leaving	

Vacation Travel Checklist (Check: Y=Yes, N=No, N/A=Not Applicable)			
Category/Description	Ck	Category/Description	Ck
Edibles		**Electronic Conveniences**	
BBQ Sauce		100 watt bulbs or 3 way blub for reading	
Bouillon cubes		A/C Adapters	
Brown sugar		Battery operated smoke detector	
Canned Peach Nectar		Cable wiring	
Canned Pinapple Juice		Camera(s)/film/Charger	
Canned Tuna		Cell phone	
Cereal Bars		Computer	
Coffee		Electric socket covers	
Cocoa/Hot chocolate packets		Extension Cord	
Concentrated juice to mix for first morning		Flashlight	
Creamer		Modular phone cord for computer	
Crystal lite		Motion detector/sensor for doorknobs	
Dried fruit and nuts		Night Lights	
Hot chocolate packets		Small car vacuum	
Hot sauce		Universal electrical adapter	
Jam/jelly		Universal TV remote control	
Ketchup		USB computer cable (to download pics from digital camera or for cable or DSL modem in room)	
Mayonnaise		White noise machine	
Mustard		**Entertainment**	
Oatmeal		Books (paperback, hardback, etc.)	
Oil-Olive/Cooking oil		CDs	
Packets of ketchup, mustard, mayo, sugar & sweetener		Color books & crayons	
Peanut butter		DVDs	
Pepper		Games	
Popcorn		Magazines	
Pop tarts		Pool and sand toys	
Salad dressing packets		Toys	
Salt		VHS casettes	

Appendix C

Vacation Travel Checklist (Check: Y=Yes, N=No, N/A=Not Applicable)			
Category/Description	Ck	**Category/Description**	Ck
Snacks		**Personal Items**	
Soda pop		Bath salts/bubble bath	
Soy sauce		Eyeglasses/contact lens/reading glasses	
Spices		Hair dryer/Hiar products	
Sugar (small container)		Mouth wash	
Tea bags		Nail clippers	
		Tooth brush & paste	
Medical		**Kitchen Necessities**	
After bite stick		Aluminum foil	
Allergy medications		Cling	
Aloe Vera for sunburns		Clips for chip bags, twist ties	
Benadryl cream		Coffee & filters, and measuring scoop	
Bactine ointment		Cooking bags (Reynolds)	
Band-Aids		Corkscrew/wine opener/can opener	
Burn spray		Crock pot	
Chapstick/lip sunscreen		Electric Griddle	
Cold Medications		Kitchen towel	
Cotton Balls		Measuring cup/measuring spoons	
Cough Drops/cough syrup		Non-stick frying pan	
Dial soap (for wounds)		Pam cooking spray	
Disinfectant spray		Paper plates and cups	
Dramamine		Paper napkins	
First Aid Kit		Paper towels	
Gauze sponges		Plastic containers for leftovers	
Hydrocortisone cream		Plastic knives/forks/spoons	
Imodium		Potato peeler	
Insect repellent		Rice Cooker	
Iodine (can be used as a water purifier)		Rubber gloves	
Jelly fish treatment (e.g., meat tenderizer)		Sharp knife	
Mosquito repellent		Special Coffee mugs	
Neosporin		Veggie steamer	
New skin liquid		Water bottle and thermal cover	

Vacation Travel Checklist			
(Check: Y=Yes, N=No, N/A=Not Applicable)			
Category/Description	Ck	Category/Description	Ck
Pepto Bismol		Water purification tablets	
Permethrin (dilute and spritz on clothes-let dry)		Wooden utensils (Big Plastic)	
Q-tips		Zip lock bags (various sizes)	
Rubbing alcohol swabs		**Wearables**	
Steri strips		Change of clothing	
Sunscreen		Disposable raincoat	
1" roll of surgical tape		Fanny pack	
Thermometer		Junk clothes (hiking, bikes, etc.)	
Telfa sponges		Robe	
Tums		Hat	
Tweezers		Shoes (flipflops, trashable sneakers, water shoes, hiking, sandals, walking)	
Tylenol/Asperin/Ibuprofen		Sleepwear	
Witch hazel		Swimming suit (2 pair)	
		Thin gloves	
Niceties		Windbreaker	
Address book			
Baby wipes			
Backpack (cheap for hiking, purchases, etc.)			
Beach Chairs			
Beach Towels/mats			
Bikes			
Binoculars			
Collapsible cooler			
Compass			
Credit cards			
Dry bag for water sports			
Dust mite pillow cover			
Extra suitcase for souvenirs			
Glue/glue stick			
Ice packs			
Leatherman's tool			
Lotion			

Appendix C

Vacation Travel Checklist				
(Check: Y=Yes, N=No, N/A=Not Applicable)				
Category/Description		Ck	Category/Description	Ck
Niceties (Continued)				
	Maps			
	Matches (short, long, "Aim&Flame")			
	Meat thermometer			
	Mini grill (george Forman, etc.)			
	Extra pillows			
	Plastic grocery sack			
	Rubber bands			
	Scissors			
	Screwdriver and other miscellaneous tools			
	Sewing Kit			
	Shampoo & conditioner			
	Snorkel & Fins			
	Stamps			
	Swiss Army Knife			
	Tape (scotch, masking, duct, etc.)			
	Toothpicks			
	Votive candles			
	Waterproof pouch			
	Ziploc-type baggies			

APPENDIX D: Top Tourist Attractions in the USA

Appendix D

Location		Attraction	Nearby Attraction
State	**City**		
AZ		Grand Canyon Nation Park	
CA	San Francisco	Golden Gate Bridge	Alcatraz Island
CA		Yosemite National Park	
CA	Los Angeles	Hollywood Walk of Fame	The Hollywood Sign
DC	DC	White House	District Memorials
FL	Orlando	Walt Disney World	
FL		Everglades National Park	
FL		The Florida Keys	
HI	Oahu	Waikiki Beach	
IA, MT and WY		Yellowstone National Park	
LA	New Orleans	French Quarter	
MA	Boston	freedom Trail	
MN	Bloomington	Mall of America	
NC, TN		Great Smoky Mountains National Park	
NV	Las Vegas	Las Vegas strip	
NY	New York	Times Square	Statue of Liberty, Empire State Building, Central Park
NY	Niagara Falls	Niagara Falls	
SC	Charleston	Fort Sumter National Monument	
SD	Keystone	Mount Rushmore National Memorial	
TN	Nashville	Grand Ole Opry	
TX	San Antonio	The Alamo	River Walk
UT		Zion National Park	

Table title: Appendix D: Top Tourist Attractions in the USA

The Family Reunion Bible

APPENDIX E: USA Cruise Port Locations & Destinations

Appendix E

United States Cruise Port Locations and Destinations
(Excluding transportation cost to departure port)

Cruise Port Location		Destinations	Prices From (per person)
State	City		
Alabama	Mobile	Caribbean - Western	$239
Alaska	Whittier	Alaska	$599
		Alaska - Gulf of Alaska	$599
California	Long Beach (Los Angeles area)	Mexico	$174
	San Pedro (Los Angeles area)	Alaska	
		Coastal - West Coast	$299
		Hawaii	$1,298
		Mexico	$439
		Panama Canal/Central America	$1,069
	San Francisco	Alaska	$759
		Alaska - Inside Passage	
		Coastal - West Coast	$249
		Hawaii	$1,299
		Mexico	$269
		Panama Canal/Central America	$1,357
	San Diego	Coastal - West Coast	$499
		Hawaii	$1,409
		Mexico	$169
		Panama Canal/Central America	$783
Florida	Miami	Bahamas	$129
		Caribbean - Eastern	$239
		Caribbean - Southern	$559
		Caribbean - Western	$169
		Panama Canal/Central America	$804
	Port Canaveral	Bahamas	$159
		Caribbean - Eastern	$249
		Caribbean - Southern	$509
		Caribbean - Western	$355
		Panama Canal/Central America	$1,392
	Fort Lauderdale	Bahamas	$256
		Canada/New England	$1,379
		Caribbean - Eastern	$454
		Caribbean - Southern	$486
		Panama Canal/Central America	$849
		South America	$1,199
	Tampa	Caribbean - Eastern	$1,349
		Caribbean - Southern	$713
		Caribbean - Western	$219
		Panama Canal/Central America	$789
	Jacksonville	Bahamas	$219

United States Cruise Port Locations and Destinations (Excluding transportation cost to departure port)			
Cruise Port Location		**Destinations**	**Prices From (per person)**
State	**City**		
Hawaii	Honolulu	Hawaii	$1,420
Louisiana	New Orleans	Caribbean - Eastern	$444
		Caribbean - Western	$239
Maryland	Baltimore	Bahamas	$459
		Bermuda	$399
		Canada/New England	$689
		Caribbean - Eastern	$569
		Caribbean - Southern	$749
Massachusetts	Boston	Bermuda	$475
		Canada/New England	$615
New Jersey	Bayonne (Cape Liberty area)	Bahamas	$566
		Bermuda	$399
		Caribbean - Eastern	$838
		Caribbean - Southern	$736
New York	New York	Bahamas	$573
		Bermuda	$398
		Canada/New England	$409
		Caribbean - Eastern	$622
		Caribbean - Southern	$919
		Europe	$748
		Panama Canal/Central America	$713
South Carolina	Charleston	Bahamas	$259
		Caribbean - Eastern	$559
Texas	Galveston	Bahamas	$1,395
		Caribbean - Eastern	$479
		Caribbean - Western	$256
		Panama Canal/Central America	$1,029
Virginia	Norfolk	Bahamas	$499
Washington	Seattle	Alaska	$419
		Alaska - Inside Passage	$559
		Coastal - West Coast	$286

APPENDIX F: Recommended Cruise Lines

The Family Reunion Bible

Appendix F

Recommended Cruise Lines for Family Vacations - Table 2 of 2

Cruise Lines

Information Categories		Carnival	Celebrity	Disney	Holland America	Norwegian	Princess	Royal Caribbean
About		Families looking for adventure and activities, family reunions	Families looking for a contemporary large ship cruise	Families who love the magic of Disney and want a large ship	Families taking a multigenerational vacation	Voted Best Family Experience by Travel Weekly	Families that prefer a large ship and an active environment	Offering the best variety over the top experiences for the entire family
Destinations		Alaska	Alaska	Alaska	Alaska	Alaska	Alaska	Alaska
		Australia	Bahamas	Bahamas	Bermuda	Bahamas	California Coastal	Bahamas
		Bahamas	Bermuda	Bermuda	Canada and New England	Bermuda	Canada and New England	Bermuda
		Bermuda	Canada/New England	Canada	Caribbean	Canada and New England	Caribbean	Canada / New England
		Canada and New England	Caribbean	Caribbean	Hawaii	Caribbean	Hawaii	Caribbean
		Caribbean	Hawaii	Disney's Castaway Cay	Mexico	Hawaii	Mexico	Hawaii
		Hawaii	Panama Canal	Hawaii	Pacific Coast	Mexican Riviera	Panama Canal	Pacific Northwest
		Mexico		Mexico	Panama Canal	Pacific Coastal		Panama Canal
		Panama Canal		Pacific Coast		Panama Canal		
				Panama Canal				

The Family Reunion Bible

Recommended Cruise Lines for Family Vacations - Table 2 of 2

Information Categories		Cruise Lines					
		Carnival	Celebrity	Disney	Holland America	Norwegian	Princess	Royal Caribbean
Departure Ports	Baltimore							
	Charleston							
	Galveston							
	Jacksonville							
	Long Beach, CA							
	Miami, FL							
	Mobile, AL							
	New Orleans							
	New York							
	Norfolk							
	Port Canaveral							
	San Diego							
	San Francisco							
	Seattle							
	Tampa							

APPENDIX G: Bus Transportation Options

Appendix G

Long Distance US Bus Companies

Long Distance U.S. Bus Companies

Company Name	U.S. Locations	Foreign Countries Served	Amenities	Phone Number	Website Address
BoltBus	The US' northeast and west coasts	None	Wi-Fi, power outlets, restrooms, air conditioning, reclinable seats	1-877-265-8287	https://www.boltbus.com/
Coach USA	Holding company for various American transportation service providers serving more than 300 cities across North America	Canada	Reclining seats, climate control, restrooms, and DVD viewing monitors, WiFi, and in-motion satellite	1-800-877-1888	https://www.coachusa.com/
Greyhound	3,800	Canada, Mexico	Wi-Fi, power outlets, restrooms, air conditioning, reclinable seats	1-844-477-8747	https://www.greyhound.com/
Jefferson Lines	Arkansas, Iowa, Kansas, Minnesota, Missouri, Montana, Nebraska, North Dakota, South Dakota, Oklahoma, Texas, Wisconsin, and Wyoming	None	Wi-Fi, power outlets, restrooms, air conditioning, reclinable seats, bus tracker, panoramic windows, Individual climate controls	1-858-800-8898	https://www.jeffersonlines.com/
Megabus	More than 100 cities in the U.S.	Canada	restrooms, power outlets, three point seatbelts and reclining seats, panoramic windows, WiFi, movies, and TV shows	1-877-462-6342	https://us.megabus.com/

Long Distance U.S. Bus Companies (Continued)

Company Name	U.S. Locations	Foreign Countries Served	Amenities	Phone Number	Website Address
Peter Pan Bus Lines	Larger cities on the east coast between New Hampshire and Washington DC	None	Wi-Fi on most buses, power outlets on most buses, restrooms, air conditioning	1-800-343-9999	https://peterpanbus.com/
RedCoach	Major destinations in Florida (Miami, Orlando, Ft Lauderdale, etc)	None	All Classes: High-speed Wi-Fi, power outlets, restrooms, air conditioning, lap trays. First & Business Class: Reclinable leather seats (140 degrees), footrests, LCD screens. First Class only: Snack boxes.	1-877-733-0724	https://www.redcoachusa.com/
Trailways	Network of approximately 70 independent bus companies that have entered into a brand licensing agreement.	Canada	Music, movies, email, 4G LTE WiFi, 120V/USB outlests, leather seats	1-800-858-8555	https://trailways.com/

Appendix G

Mexican Bus Companies

Mexican Bus Companies Offering Cross-Border Transportation Between U.S. and Mexico

Company Name	U.S. Cities Served	Amenities	Phone Number	Website Address
El Expreso	Illinois, Florida, Georgia, Arkansas, Tennessee, North and South Carolina and Alabama and within Texas from Houston	Power outlets, USB plugs, air conditioning	1-800-601-6559	https://www.busbud.com/en/bus-company/el-expreso
El Paso Los Angeles Limousine Express	El Paso, Los Angeles, Phoenix, Denver, Las Cruces, Albuquerque	WiFi on selected buses, wide reclining seats, large scenic windows, air conditioning, heated, restroom, TV, DVD	1-866-691-9732	https://eplalimo.com/home
Omnibus Express	Texas, Florida, Kentucky, Georgia, Louisiana	TV, wide seats, air conditioning (Omnibus Express, Omex Primera); TV, wide seats, air conditioning, outlets, audio, footrest, WiFi, Snack (Omex VIP)	01-800-765-66-36 (MX), +1-800-923-1799 (US)	https://omnibusexpress.com/en/
Tufesa	Los Angeles, Sacramento, Bakersfield, Fresno, Salt Lake City, Barstow, Las Vegas, St George, Phoenix, Tucson, Nogales, San Francisco, San Diego	Power plugs, air conditioning, movies, restroom	1-702-254-6899 1-213-489-8079	http://www.tufesabus.com/
Turimex Internacional	Texas, Illinois, North Carolina, South Carolina, Louisiana, Michigan, Mississippi, arkansas, Tennessee, Alabama, Georgia	Air conditioning, restroom power outlet, WiFi	1-800-980-108 (US), 01-800-881-8181 (MX)	https://www.turimex.com/en/

Charter Bus Companies

Charter Bus Companies For Family Reunions

Company Name	Number of Passengers	Amenities	Phone Number	Website Address
Bus	Up to 56	Reclining seats, reading lights, individual climate control, LED flat screen monitors, AM/FM stereo, DVD player, PA system, restroom, panoramic windows, window shades, overhead and undercarriage storage	1-214-748-5466	https://bususa.net/family-reunions.html
Cardinal Bus	Up to 56	WiFi, 110 outlets, reclining seats, AM/FM stereo/CD players, PA system, climate control, restrooms, DVD players	1-800-348-7487	https://www.cardinalbuses.com/motorcoach-services/charter-bus-for-family-reunion/
Champion Coach	Up to 56	GPS tracking, comfortable seating, large viewing windows, enhanced lighting, wide screen monitors, WiFi, 110v outlets, wireless microphone, restrooms	1-800-583-7668	https://championcoach.com/group-travel/family-reunion-travel/
Citbus	Up to 60	High back cushioned reclining seats, reading lights, overhead luggage compartments, USB outlets, air conditioning and heating, restrooms, WiFi, DVD players	1-515-233-0286	https://citbus.com/family-reunions/
Coach USA	Call	Reclining seats, individual climate control, personal fans, restrooms, WiFi, power outlets, TV	See website	https://www.coachusa.com/charters/family-reunion-charter-bus

Appendix G

Charter Bus Companies For Family Reunions (Continued)

Company Name	Number of Passengers	Amenities	Phone Number	Website Address
National Charter Bus	Up to 56	WiFi, TV, DVD players, restrooms	1-317-735-6979	https://www.nationalbuscharter.com/personal-trip-bus-rental
Superior Tours	Up to 56	WiFi, electrical outlets, laptrays, 6 DVD screens, window shades, footrests, restroom, seatbelts	1-800-754-9097	http://superiortours.com/family-reunions/
US Coachways	Up to 57	Wifi, DVD players, stereo and PA systems, and charging stations, bathrooms	1-855-473-5969	https://www.uscoachways.com/family-reunion
Village Travel	Up to 56	Call	1-800-333-0312	https://villagetours.net/reunion-charter-bus/
WindStar	Up to 56	High back reclining seats, DVD, TV, GPS, individual climate control, under-floor luggage capacity, overhead storage, restroom, PA system, 110 volt outlets, WiFi	1-888-494-6378	https://gowindstar.com/family-reunions.html

APPENDIX H: Sample Costs to Rent Owner Timeshares vs From Resort

Appendix H

Appendix H Sample Cost Comparison to Rent Owner Timeshares vs From Resort*

Resort Name	Location	Rental Month	Total Retal Site Price For The Week (2 Bedrooms)			
			Resort Site	Airbnb	VRBO	Redweek
Harborside at Atlantis	Bahamas	December	$5,900	$4,900	$4,804	$3,200
Marriott Grande Ocean	Hilton Head Island, SC	June	$5,300	$3,990	$5,400	$2,900
Hyatt Sunset Harbor	Key West, FL	December	No availability	$7,300	$7,085	$2,600
Wyndham Long Wharf	Newport, RI	July	$5,055	$3,900	$6,091	$1,900
Westin St John	St. John, USVI	December	$4,500	$5,300	$5,400	$3,800
Tortuga Beach Club	Sanibel Island, FL	March	$2,400	$6,900	$4,800	$2,300
Marriott's Newport Coast	Newport Coast, CA	June	$4,200	$3,900	$4,100	$2,300
Hilton Lagoon Tower	Honolulu, HI	June	$4,500	$4,800	$4,700	$3,300

*Prices seen on 3/27/2021

APPENDIX I: Popular US Festivals

Appendix I

Popular U.S. Festivals*

Location		Festival Name	Month	Website
State	City			
GA	Atlanta	Afropunk Fest Atlanta	Oct	https://afropunk.com/
NY	New York	Afropunk Fest Brooklyn	Aug	https://afropunk.com/
NM	Albuquerque	Albuquerque International Balloon Fiesta	Oct	https://balloonfiesta.com/
HI	Honolulu	Aloha Festival	Mar	https://www.alohafestivals.com/
TX	Austin	Austin City Limits Music Festival	Oct	https://www.aclfestival.com/
TN	Manchester	Bonnaroo Music and Arts Festival	Jun/Jul	https://www.bonnaroo.com/
NV	Black Rock Desert	Burning Man Festival	Aug	https://burningman.org/
WY	Cheyenne	Cheyenne Frontier Days	Jul	https://www.cfdrodeo.com/
CA	Indio	Coachella Valley Music And Arts Festival	Apr	https://www.coachella.com/
CA	Moreno Beach	Desert Daze Festival	Oct	https://desertdaze.ca/
NV	Las Vegas	Electric Daisy Carnival	May	https://lasvegas.electricdaisycarnival.com/
MI	Rothbury	Electric Forest	Jun/Jul	https://electricforestfestival.com/
LA	New Orleans	Essence Music Festival	Jul	https://www.essence.com/
FL	Key West	Fantasy Fest	Oct	https://www.fantasyfest.com/
DE	Dover	Firefly Music Festival	Jun	https://fireflyfestival.com/
NJ	East Rutherford	Hot 97 Summer Jam	Jun	https://www.hot97.com/
FL	Miami	III Points Music Festival	Oct	https://www.iiipoints.com
GA	Macon	International Cherry Blossom Festival	Mar/Apr	https://cherryblossom.com/
LA	New Orleans	Jazz And Heritage Festival	Apr/May	https://www.noiazzfest.com/
PA	Kutztown	Kutztown Folk Festival	Jun/Jul	https://www.kutztownfestival.com/
IL	Chicago	Lollapalooza	Jul/Aug	https://www.lollapalooza.com/

The Family Reunion Bible

Popular U.S. Festivals*

Location		Festival Name	Month	Website
State	**City**			
ME	Rockland	Maine Lobster Festival	Aug	https://www.mainelobsterfestival.com/
LA	New Orleans	Mardi Gras	Feb	https://www.neworleans.com/
IL	Chicago	Pitchfork Music Festival	Jul	https://pitchforkmusicfestival.com/
FL	Miami	Rolling Loud Festival	Feb	https://www.rollingloud.com/miami
OR	Ashland	Shakespeare Festival	Varies	https://www.osfashland.org/
TX	Austin	South By SouthWest (SXSW)	Mar	https://www.sxsw.com/festivals/music/
CA	Indio	Stagecoach Festival	Apr	https://tasteofcountry.com
UT	Park City	Sundance Film Fest	Jan/Feb	https://www.sundance.org/
NY	New York	The Governors Ball Music Festival	Jun/Jul	https://www.governorsballmusicfestival.com/

*All festivals, locations and dates subject to change

APPENDIX J: DNA Testing Company Comparisons

Appendix J

DNA Testing company Comparisons

Company Name	Pros	Cons
Family Tree DNA	Competitive pricing for DNA Autosomnal test	Database (766,000+ people) isn't quite as large as other services
	Only site to offer Autosomal DNA, Y-DNA and mtDNA testing kits	
	Website supports targeted DNA genealogical projects	
	Stores your DNA sample for 25 years	
	Provides trusted privacy for your test sample	
	You receive email addresses for your genetic matches	
	Chromosome browser tool to compare shared chromosomal segments	
	Allows uploading of raw DNA results from 23andMe, Ancestry DNA and Geno 2.0	
	Excellent online community forums and customer service	
	Provides biogeographical ancestry analysis	
Ancestry DNA	Competitive pricing for Autosomnal DNA test	No targeted genealogical DNA projects available to join on website
	Largest database – 1.4 million people	Can't upload raw DNA data from other services
	Reliable security for DNA test samples and results	No chromosome browser
	Excellent online community forums and customer service	
	Provides biogeographical ancestry analysis	
	Stores your DNA sample indefinitely	
	Can connect with genetic matches via anonymous email and message boards	
National Geographic Geno 2.0	Offers autosomnal and full mtDNA testing (but limited Y-DNA)	DNA test is expensive
	Test samples saved securely for privacy	Much smaller database at 200,000 (but you can upload to FTDNA)
	Contributing to a globally targeted genealogical DNA project	Can't upload raw DNA data from other services
	Excellent online community forums and customer service	No chromosome browser
	Provides biogeographical ancestry analysis	No website support for connecting with genetic matches
23andMe	Large database of 1 million people	Very expensive pricing for DNA Autosomal test
	Test samples and results are secure for privacy	Harder to connect with genetic matches
	Provides chromosome browser to compare shared chromosomal segments	No genealogical DNA projects available to join on website
	Provides biogeographical ancestry analysis	Can't upload raw DNA data from other services
	Stores your DNA sample	Genealogical community forums are lacking

APPENDIX K: Award Certificate Samples

Family Reunion Award
Location/Date

- **AWARD CERTIFICATE**

This certificate is awarded to:
_____

For being the First To pay Lodging Fees

Henry Thomas
Reunion Chairman

Alma Bates
Reunion Co-Chairwoman

Family Reunion Award
Location/Date

• AWARD CERTIFICATE

This certificate is awarded to:

_____

For being the First to Arrive

Henry Thomas
Reunion Chairman

Alma Bates
Reunion Co-Chairwoman

Appendix K

Family Reunion Award
Location/Date

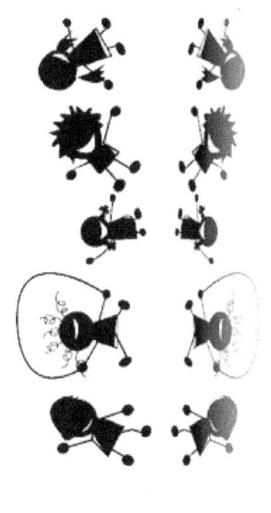

· **AWARD CERTIFICATE**

This certificate is awarded to:

_____

For having the Most Children Present

Henry Thomas
Reunion Chairman

Alma Bates
Reunion Co-Chairwoman

165

Family Reunion Award

Location/Date

- **AWARD CERTIFICATE**

This certificate is awarded to:

_____

For having the Most Keys

Henry Thomas
Reunion Chairman

Alma Bates
Reunion Co-Chairwoman

Family Reunion Award
Location/Date

- **AWARD CERTIFICATE**

This certificate is awarded to:

_____

For having Lived in the Most Places

Henry Thomas
Reunion Chairman

Alma Bates
Reunion Co-Chairwoman

Family Reunion Award
Location/Date

• AWARD CERTIFICATE

This certificate is awarded to:
_____

For having the Most Degrees

Henry Thomas
Reunion Chairman

Alma Bates
Reunion Co-Chairwoman

Appendix K

Family Reunion Award
Location/Date

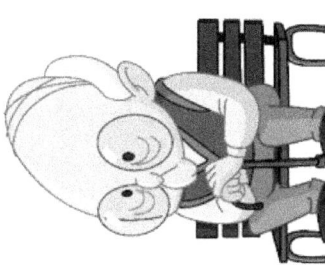

- **AWARD CERTIFICATE**

This certificate is awarded to:

_____

For being the Oldest

Henry Thomas
Reunion Chairman

Alma Bates
Reunion Co-Chairwoman

169

Family Reunion Award

Location/Date

• AWARD CERTIFICATE

This certificate is awarded to:

_____

Bowling Winner

Henry Thomas
Reunion Chairman

Alma Bates
Reunion Co-Chairwoman

Appendix K

Family Reunion Award
Location/Date

- **AWARD CERTIFICATE**

This certificate is awarded to:

_____

Card Game Winner

Henry Thomas
Reunion Chairman

Alma Bates
Reunion Co-Chairwoman

Family Reunion Award

Location/Date

• AWARD CERTIFICATE

This certificate is awarded to:

_____

For being the Grand Prize Winner*!

*The winner has won one week of lodging in Orlando (in a 1 bedroom timeshare)! Blackout dates may apply. Certificate must be used by June 24, 2018. A $100 confirmation fee applies.

Henry Thomas
Reunion Chairman

Alma Bates
Reunion Co-Chairwoman

APPENDIX L: Sample Vacation Reference Charts

Appendix L

Orlando Vacation Reference Charts

Appendix L

Family Vacation
Orlando, FL

Date

The Family Reunion Bible

Orlando

Topics

- Welcome
- Theme
- Accomplishments/milestones/awards
- Logistics
  - People locations
  - Meeting places
  - Videotaping
  - Guest book
  - Gift Bags
  - Income and expenses
- Orientation
  - Resort layout
  - Attractions/things to do/festivals
  - Restaurants and grocery stores
  - Shopping (outlet malls, etc.)
  - Nightlife venues
- Family reunion itinerary
  - Games/contests
  - Optional activities

Welcome

- Welcome to the Family Reunion!
- Organizers

The Family Reunion Bible

Orlando

Reunion Theme: *Discover Our Roots*

- Roots Topics
    - Genealogy overview
    - Our ancestors
    - Our racial mixture
    - Discovered cousins
    - Tracing family history

Accomplishments/ Milestones/Awards

- Graduations

- Graduations

The Family Reunion Bible

Orlando

Accomplishments/ Milestones/Awards

Births

Marriages

Retirements

Appendix L

Accomplishments/ Milestones/Awards

Accomplishments

The Family Reunion Bible

Orlando

Accomplishments/ Milestones/Awards

- Awards (Awards printed)
  - First to pay reunion lodging fees – Larry
  - First to arrive for reunion
  - Who has the most children present?
  - Who has the most grandchildren present?
  - Who has the most keys on their keyring?
  - Who has the longest name?
  - Who has lived in the most places?
  - Who has the most degrees?
  - Who is the oldest?
  - Who is the youngest?
  - Person attending for the first time

In Memory of

The Family Reunion Bible

Orlando

People Locations
Resort People Reside At

- **HGVC Tuscany Village**
  8122 Arrezzo Way
  Orlando, FL 32821
  (407) 465-2600
  ➤ Unit #: _____
     - _____ People
  ➤ Unit #: _____
     - _____ People

- **Grand Beach**
  8317 Lake Bryan Beach Boulevard
  Orlando, FL 32821
  407-238-2500
  ➤ Unit #: _____
  ➤ Unit #: _____

- **Wyndham Bonnet Creek**
  9560 Via Encinas
  Lake Buena Vista, FL 32830
  407-238-3500

Appendix L

People Locations
Which Resort Are People In?

- **Marriott's Grande Vista**
  5925 Avenida Vista
  Orlando, FL 32821
  407-238-7676
  - Unit #: _____
    - _____ People
  - Unit #: _____
    - _____ People

- **Oasis Lakes at The Fountains**
  12400 International Drive
  Orlando, FL, USA, 32821
  407/905-4100
  - Unit #: _____
    - _____ People

- **Sheraton Vistana**
  8800 Vistana Centre Dr
  Orlando, FL 32821
  (407) 239-3100

Resorts Overview Map

Orlando

Meeting Places

- Orientation
  - Sunday
  - Location
- Indoor games
  - Locations to be determined during reunion
- Outdoor games
  - Location
- Family history briefing
  - Location
- Potluck dinner
  - Location
- Video of current and previous reunions
  - Location

Videotaping/Pictures

- Who will be videotaping/picture-taking POC?
  - Please plan on sharing your pictures/videos
  - What is the cost per person? (DVDs, etc.)
  - Picture album will be generated and passed to participants
    - Via DVD, email, etc.
- Who will generate video of previous reunions?

Guest Book

- Guest book is available for attendees to sign
  - Name
  - Home address
  - Email address
- The books from each reunion will be available for review at future reunions.
- Bring last year's book
- Alma to find book for this reunion to input sheets in

Family Reunion Gift Bags

Orlando

- Tote bags were ordered from rhodeislandnovelty.com
- Magnets
- Personalized pencils
- Personalized pens
- 4"x6" note pads – 45 sheets (use logo from T-shirts)
- Get pamphlets locally
- Gift bag cover sheets()
  - Checking to see if pattern from T-shirts can be put on bags – Cost is $2.50 per page
- Folders to put papers (bookmark, these charts, etc.)?
- Personalized candle holders (one color)
- Florida Powerball ticket (Wednesday, June 28 drawing – need to purchase Sunday)
  - Generate spreadsheet with each person's lottery number before putting in bag

Appendix L

Family Reunion Gift Bags

Get pamphlets locally
- International Drive Trolley map

Orlando

I-RIDE Trolley Service

What is the I-RIDE Trolley Service?
The I-RIDE Trolley is the exclusive, convenient and affordable transportation to hundreds of exciting destinations within the International Drive Resort area.

When Does the I-RIDE Trolley Operate?
Daily from 8:00 a.m. to 10:30 p.m.

Where Does the I-RIDE Trolley Go?
The I-RIDE Trolleys travel exclusively throughout the International Drive Resort area.

The Red Line Trolley route services the International Drive both north and south bound. Red Line trolleys arrive approximately every 20 minutes.

The Green Line Trolley route is the counterpart to the Red Line Trolley route, beginning service in the Major Boulevard business district, travels along Universal Boulevard and then shadows the Red Line Trolley route on South International Drive. Green Line trolleys arrive approximately every 30 minutes.

Refer to the I-RIDE Trolley route map for specific locations of Red Line and Green Line stops.

I-RIDE Trolley Service

- **Cash Fare**
  - Single fare is $2.00 per ride
  - Child fare $1.00 per ride (ages 3 to 9 with paying adult)
  - Senior citizen (65 and over) fare is $0.25 per ride
  - Exact change is required
  - Drivers do not carry cash
  - Passes not sold on trolleys
- **Unlimited Ride Passes**
  - One-Day Pass: $5.00 per person
  - Three-Day Pass: $7.00 per person
  - Five-Day Pass: $9.00 per person
  - Seven-Day Pass: $12.00 per person
- **Online Pass Purchase**
  - http://www.iridetrolley.com/store/index.asp
- **Pass Sales Locations**
  - http://www.iridetrolley.com/passes.asp

The Family Reunion Bible

Personalized Candle Holder Front and Back Picture

Orlando

Thomas Family Vacation
Orlando, FL
June 2017

Personalized Pens & Pencils

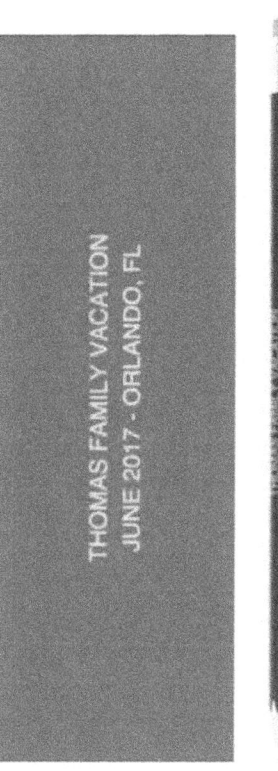

The Family Reunion Bible

Orlando

Family Reunion Display Table

- Table showing previous T-shirts, and other items from old reunions.
  - Lee to reserve table in Orlando from resorts or rent one.
- Have attendees bring their family memorabilia, pictures, etc., to show off?
  - Take pictures so we can scan the items for storage
- Display all the game prizes on table.

TABLE RENTALS

8 Ft Table (Seats 8/10) **$10.00**

60" Round Table (Seats 8-10) **$11.00**

6 Foot Rectangle Table (Seats 6-8) **$9.00**

Attractions/Things to Do/Festivals

- One of the newer must-do attractions of International Drive is the Leonardo DaVinci exhibit. Here you get to explore one of the world's most brilliant minds. Discover the genius works of art, engineering and science. Explore some of the authentic recreations of some of his most magnificent work.
- Discover the impossibly scenic oasis that is **Orlando Wetlands Park** (25155 Wheeler Road, Christmas, **orlandowetlands.org**), a breathtaking wildlife preserve and one of Central Florida's most picturesque parks.
- Take the **Winter Park Scenic Boat Tour** (312 E. Morse Blvd., Winter Park; **scenicboattours.com**), which takes you through an amazing series of lush, narrow canals that connect the Winter Park Chain of Lakes. If you've ever wondered whether this tour was worth checking out, the answer is yes – do it.
- Get permission to paint the Pho Hoa wall (649 N. Primrose Drive; phohoaorlandofl.com), a community canvas that blends graffiti artists of all experience levels to form a colorful local conversation piece.

The Family Reunion Bible

Attractions/Things to Do/Festivals

Orlando

- **Escapology Orlando** brings a new kind of entertainment to Orlando with its first US location. The attraction challenges guests to be their own heroes in a thrilling game of adventure and mystery. Teams of up to six players are locked in a themed room with just 60 minutes to combine clues, solve puzzles and discover the key to escape.
- **Bite30** is Orlando's 30-Day Restaurant Week, featuring the best local restaurants and chefs driving Orlando's culinary scene. From June 1 to 30, participating restaurants offer special prix fixe menus that offer multicourse lunches or dinners at a set price ($15 for lunch, $30 for dinner). Diners get the opportunity to try multiple dishes on the restaurant's menu for about the cost of a single entree, and restaurants get to showcase their specialty dishes to the new customers attracted by the Bite30 menu! Restaurant-hop through the City Beautiful, experience delicious food, service and ambiance of the restaurants you really should know about.
(Look for Bite Night date)
http://bite30.com/

Appendix L

Attractions/Things to Do/Festivals

- **The Walt Disney World Theme Parks**
  - Four theme parks (Magic Kingdom, the top place for those with little kids), EPCOT, Disney's Hollywood Studios, and Animal Kingdom)
  - Two excellent water parks

Ticket Source/Website	1-Day Price	3-Day Price (w/hopper)	4-Day with hopper
Disney https://disneyworld.disney.go.com/tickets/	$124.00		
Undercover Tourist http://www.undercovertourist.com	$96.97	$307.85 ($359.81)	$343.97 ($413.27)
Official Ticket Center http://www.officialticketcenter.com	$116.83	$305.75 ($359.00)	$343.00 ($410.00)

- **Universal Orlando Resort**
  - A complex of rides, attractions and theme areas divided into two parks, Universal Studios Florida and Universal's Islands of Adventures. Universal also owns and operates Wet 'n' Wild, the area's original water park.

Attractions/Things to Do/Festivals
Orlando/Disney Related Links

Orlando

- http://www.undercovertourist.com/
- http://www.orlandomagazine.com/Orlando-Magazine/May-2013/2013-Dining-Awards/
- http://www.disboards.com/
- http://allears.net/index.html
- http://www.orlandotouristinformationbureau.com/
- http://www.visitorlando.com/things-to-do/free-things-to-do/
- http://travel.nationalgeographic.com/travel/city-guides/free-orlando-traveler/
- http://www.hotels.com/articles/ar000520/top-10-free-things-to-do-in-orlando/
- http://www.orlandoinformer.com/universal/20-ideas-for-free-or-inexpensiveentertainmentaround-orlando/
- http://www.smartdestinations.com/blog/8-free-things-to-do-in-orlando/
- http://traveltips.usatoday.com/fun-things-orlando-20774.html
- http://www.ytravelblog.com/what-to-do-in-orlando/
- http://eventjunkies.net/40-things-to-do-in-central-florida/

Appendix L

Attractions/Things to Do/Festivals

- **Harry P. Leu Gardens**
  - Leu Gardens is a botanical charmer.
  - The Leu House, built in 1888, is surrounded by 40 acres of formal gardens.
- **Fantasy of Flight**
  - Located a half hour southeast of Walt Disney World, this is Orlando's answer to the National Air + Space Museum.
- **Downtown Disney**
  - They have Circus du Solei, Lego land, Disney Quest, AMC Dine-in theater, House of Blues and many cool shops and restaurants.
- **Universal CityWalk**
  - CityWalk has a great nightlife.
- **Discovery Cove**
  - a beautiful, tropical oasis.
- **Wishes Fireworks**
  - Explosive display of fireworks over the Magic Kingdom.

Orlando

Attractions/Things to Do/Festivals

- **iFly Orlando**
  - The closest thing to skydiving you'll ever do without having to jump out of an airplane.
- **Gatorland**
  - Features 3,000 gators and 89 crocodiles, as well as a number of bird and snake exhibits.
- **Wet N' wild**
  - If you have kids and teenagers on your vacation, they can easily spend 2 or 3 days here enjoying the sun and water slides.
- **Ripley's Orlando**
  - For less than $20, you can spend about two hours walking through the Orlando edition of Ripley's Believe It Or Not.
- **Orlando Science Center**
  - This is an excellent vacation day for kids and one of the few cheap things to do in Orlando.
- **Kissimmee Air Museum**
  - The planes here aren't behind sheets of glass, or even ropes or gates. You can get up close and take excellent pictures of the exhibits at the Kissimmee Air Museum.

Appendix L

- **Titanic The Experience**
  - This unique Titanic museum offers an amazing opportunity to tour a replica, with actors dressed in period costumes working as tour guides to enhance the experience.
- **Forever Florida EcoSafaris**
  - Journey deep into the 4,700-acre Forever Florida wildlife conservation area. Coach Safari, Horseback Safari or soar through the treetops on the Zipline Safari.
- **Old Town Kissimmee**
  - If you're looking for some shopping, dining, and entertainment opportunities, Old Town is a good place to go. There are a lot of cool shops and fun rides for kids. Admission is free and parking is free.
- **Kennedy Space Center Visitor Complex, Orlando**
- **SeaWorld Orlando**
  - Sea World comprises three separate attractions: Sea World, Discovery Cove and Aquatica.
- **Orlando Museum of Art**

The Family Reunion Bible

Orlando

Attractions/Things to Do/Festivals
Free Things to Do

Arts & Culture

- The Zora Neale Hurston National Museum of Fine Arts takes you on a stroll through history, starting with the author's humble beginnings and displays creative works of other artists of African descent. Donations are accepted.
- The Holocaust Memorial Resource and Education Center of Florida presents an overview of the history of the Holocaust and serves as a memorial to victims. The center also hosts many educational events, films and seminars. Donations are accepted.
- The Winter Park Historical Museum houses a photo timeline of the history of Winter Park and features changing themed exhibits.
- CityArts Factory is an eclectic collection of art galleries in downtown Orlando showcasing local and international artists. Free admission Tuesday through Saturday from 11 a.m. to 6 p.m.
- The Grand Bohemian Gallery in Orlando has two locations in downtown Orlando and Celebration. Both feature a variety of art, including jewelry, glass and sculpture.
- The Fred Stone Theatre at Rollins College has a student-produced "Second Stage Series" that is free. Evening performances are Wednesday to Saturday, with matinees on Saturday and Sunday. The shows are general admission and the audience is seated on a first come, first served basis.
- Albin Polasek Museum and Sculpture Gardens. Not only are the museum and gardens free, but you'll also find a scattering around the grounds of artists creating new works.

Attractions/Things to Do/Festivals

Free Things to Do

Arts & Culture (Continued)

- The Leu Botanical Gardens (leugardens.org) on the banks of Lake Rowena feature 50 acres of tropical beauty. On Mondays in the summer it's free (other days its $10 for adults, $3 for kids under 18).

The Family Reunion Bible

Orlando

Attractions/Things to Do/Festivals

Free Things to Do

Parks & Nature

- Black Hammock Adventures on Lake Jessup offers free live alligator and bird exhibits. At the Lazy Gator Bar, guests can join the deck party every Friday and Saturday night and listen to free, live music.
- Called Central Florida's "secret garden," the 5.22-acre Kraft Azalea Gardens is located on Lake Maitland in Winter Park and open from 8 a.m. to dusk. Most of all, it's free.
- University of Central Florida's Arboretum is home to more than 600 plant species on an 80-acre property. Visitors can walk through a self-guided tour to view an impressive number of native plant species.
- The Winter Park Farmer's Market is held from 7 a.m. to 1 p.m. every Saturday. Local vendors and farmers sell their homemade and homegrown specialties, including fruits, vegetables, organic produce, baked goods and more.
- Lake Eola Park is a 43-acre recreational area in the heart of downtown Orlando. Visitors can picnic along the shore, enjoy one of the many free concerts at the amphitheater, feed the resident swans or stop by the farmer's market on Sundays.
- Take a free yoga class at Lake Eola on Sundays, because your dog could be a little more downward.
- Fort Christmas Historical Park is a little slice of old Florida. Visit the fort, the historical homes on-site and the gift shop.
- Big Tree Park in Sanford features 11 acres of natural vegetation and wetlands.
- Camp out and roast marshmallows with Disney characters Chip n' Dale at Disney's Fort Wilderness Resort for free. The evening sing-along around the campfire includes a viewing of a Disney movie. Starts at 7:30 p.m.

Attractions/Things to Do/Festivals

Free Things to Do

- **Food & Wine**
- Lakeridge Winery & Vineyards, which sits on 80 breathtaking acres just north of Orlando, offers free tours, tastings and many free festivals and events.
- The Orlando Brewing Company near downtown Orlando is the only organic brewery and taproom in the Southeast and one of only 10 in the United States. Each weekend, there are free brewery tours, free Wi-Fi and free live entertainment.
- Opened in 1935 in Orlando, Chamberlin's Market & Cafe is more than an organic grocery store. Stop by for free classes and guest speakers year-round.

Attractions/Things to Do/Festivals

Free Things to Do

Orlando

Music

- All Orlando visitors can enjoy free nightly Italian music performances at the picturesque Portofino Bay Hotel at Universal Orlando's piazza (weather permitting). The hotel has been recognized as one of the most elaborate themed hotel environments in the United States.
- Natura Coffee and Tea.
- This small cafe has live performances every night, usually starting around 9 p.m. Check out jazz on Wednesdays, a general open mic on Thursdays, and acoustic and spoken-word open mics on Sundays.
- See a show at the Timucua Arts White House (2000 S. Summerlin Ave.; timucua.com). This unique music venue is located in the home of local musician Benoit Glazer and his family, but they have transformed it into an acoustically pleasing, fully functional venue with three tiers of seating. Most shows are free, but you're expected to bring a bottle of wine to share. A pittance for such a gorgeous experience – every Sunday night.

Attractions/Things to Do/Festivals

Free Things to Do

Miscellaneous

- LEGO Imagination Center at downtown Disney Marketplace is 4,400-square feet of fun. Guarded by friendly dinosaurs and a huge sea serpent made of LEGO bricks, this play area lets kids explore their creativity by building with colorful bricks, and it's all free.
- Disney's Boardwalk features free, live street entertainment in the evenings, including comedians, jazz ensembles and fire shows.
- Each year, thousands of tourists who visit Orlando go to Lake Wales, Florida, to see if the old Indian Legend of Spook Hill is true. A sign marks the spot where you should stop your car, put it in neutral, and watch as your car rolls uphill.
- Just south of the Orlando International Airport is Old Town, a unique amusement park and shopping area. Old Town comes to life on Saturdays with a vintage-car parade starting at 1 p.m. On Wednesday evenings, The Dukes, a '50s and '60s cover band, play doo-wop hits and lead the crowd in the Stroll, the line dance made famous on *American Bandstand*. Visitors must buy tickets for the amusement rides, but admission to Old Town, and its concerts and car shows, is free.
- Popcorn Flicks in Central Park.
- Popcorn Flicks is a series of outdoor movies starting at 8 p.m. throughout the summer in Winter Park.

The Family Reunion Bible

Orlando

Attractions/Things to Do/Festivals
Free Things to Do

Miscellaneous (Continued)

- Universal Orlando Resorts City Walk.
- This is a free part of Universal where you can see some sidewalk attractions and enjoy the studio without having to go into the amusement park. Come early to snag free parking.
- Mall at Millenia.
- One of Orlando's enduring charms is its weather, a feature taken advantage of on a weekly basis at the Enzian Theater during its Wednesday Night Pitcher Show. Yes, that is a play on words but no, the beer isn't free. The movie is, though, and shown outside under the stars, surrounded by the centuries-old live oaks standing sentinel around the property. The Enzian's Eden Bar is on hand for drinks soft and hard and its kitchen is open for eats, but if you're handy with film trivia, you might win yourself a Jell-O shot. Bring chairs, blankets, friends and family and enjoy the features, which range from classic to kitsch, suspense to sci-fi. Check the Enzian's website for what's playing. (407-629-0054, 407-629-1088)
- Baldwin Park is a newer, upscale area just a few miles from downtown Orlando. Here you will find beautiful homes and landscaping, lots of stores and dining, and a handful of nice parks. Lake Baldwin Park features a two-and-a-half-mile trail around the lake, perfect for bike riding or walking in the early morning hours before it gets too hot.

Appendix L

Attractions/Things to Do/Festivals
Free Things to Do

- Pick up a Free City Guide for great coupon deals. Orlando has three major city-wide guides, and they are all free. This is the best place to find great buy one get one free coupons, as well as great drink specials.
- Ship all the purchases home and save. We suggest you tell the sales clerk that you want the items to be shipped to your house, especially if you live out of state. This will save you the hassle of having to pack all your new items and you will also save on the 6.5% sales tax (essentially you will be getting your items shipped home for free).
- Visitors should check with their designated hotel ahead of time to determine if shuttle service is provided to and from theme parks and the airport.
- The I-Ride Trolley offers an easy and economical way to explore the International Drive resort area without a car. Visitors can hop on and off the I-Ride Trolley, which makes stops at a number of hotels and attractions on International Drive.

The Family Reunion Bible

Attractions/Things to Do/Festivals
Tips

Orlando

- Don't take bags to the parks. You will save time not having to have them checked or put in lockers.
- Visit Orlando offers the Magicard, a free pass good for a constantly changing roster of discounts on everything from museum admission to restaurant dining. You can pick them up at the visitors' center, but save time by printing one online or ordering one that will come in the mail.
- For visitors to downtown Orlando, a free circulating bus called LYMMO provides rides along a 3-mile loop in the downtown area. Service is provided every five minutes during office hours and every ten minutes in the evenings. See their website for daily schedules.
- Visit Orlando App
  - Personalized recommendations
  - Search area maps
  - Purchase discount tickets
  - Play fun games
  - Connect with a Visit Orlando Destination Specialist
  - Available from Google Play or Apple App Store

Appendix L

Attractions/Things to Do/Festivals
Day Trips

- Bok Tower Gardens in Lake Wales, Florida – This majestic 200-acre garden features a 205-foot singing tower facing a reflecting pool, a bird sanctuary, and acres of oaks, pines, ferns, camellias, jasmine, spider lily, and wetland plants.
- Silver Springs State Park in Ocala is famous for it's glass-bottom boat rides, one of Florida's oldest tourist attractions. Here you will have an opportunity to take an exciting narrated ride across the largest artesian springs formation in the world. The transparent bottom of the boat allows you to see all different types of fish and plant life. Be sure to keep an eye out for the occasional gator sighting on the banks. The beautiful Spanish moss trees surrounding the lake make for an incredibly scenic ride. Bring with your camera – there are plenty of fantastic photo opportunities at this beautiful state park.
  Approximate Driving Time: 1 hour and 15 minutes.
- Explore the striking grounds and Mayan Revival buildings of Orange County's first National Historic Landmark, the **Maitland Art Center** (231 E. Packwood Ave., Maitland; **<u>artandhistory.org</u>**).

Attractions/Things to Do/Festivals
Day Trips (Continued)

Orlando

- **Kennedy Space Center Visitor Complex**
State Road 405, Kennedy Space Center, Florida
321-449-4444 http://www.kennedyspacecenter.com/
- **Canaveral National Seashore**
Canaveral National Seashore Information Center
7611 South Atlantic Avenue, New Smyrna Beach, Florida
321-267-1110 http://www.nps.gov/cana/index.htm
- **Lakeridge Winery & Vineyards**
19239 U.S. 27 North, Clermont, Florida
352-394-8627, 1-800-768-9463 http://www.lakeridgewinery.com/
- **Sterling Casino Lines** Contact Information Address: 817 N Atlantic Ave Cocoa Beach, FL 32931 Phone Number: 3217832212
- **Suncruise Casino** Contact Information Address: 405 Atlantis Rd Cape Canaveral, FL 32920 Phone Number: 3217838302
- **Victory Casino Cruises**: 180 Christopher Columbus Drive, Cape Canaveral, FL 32920, (855) 468-4286

Attractions/Things to Do/Festivals
Day Trips (Continued)

- The closest beaches to Orlando are Cocoa Beach, Canaveral National Seashore and Daytona Beach, all about an hour and a half drive away. Cocoa Beach can be reached via Toll Road 528 and Canaveral National Seashore can be accessed by taking SR 50 east to US1. Daytona Beach can be accessed via Interstate 4 (I-4) East.
- Florida's tranquil West Coast beaches, including St. Pete Beach, Clearwater Beach and Tarpon Springs, are only about a two hours' drive away via Interstate 4.

The Family Reunion Bible

Orlando

Attractions/Things to Do/Festivals

Orlando's Breathtaking Freshwater Springs

Blue Springs

- As the largest spring on the St. John's River, **Blue Springs is well recognized for its beautiful translucent water**, live oak trees leaning blissfully over the run and adorable manatee population (the designated Manatee Refuge houses hundreds of the gentle giants in the winter season). Viewing boardwalks and overlooks along the spring provide striking views of the awe-inspiring creatures. Boat tours, canoeing and kayaking, cabins and campgrounds, trails for hiking and underwater diving caves are just a few activities you won't want to miss here.

De Leon Springs

- Named after Spanish explorer Ponce De Leon, who is said to have passed through the area, these springs stay at a perfect 72 degrees year-round. Spot native wildlife like white-tailed deer, alligators, otters, turtles, kingfishers and American bald eagles at this secluded park. Enjoy active relaxation with canoeing, kayaking, fishing and swimming, plus a hiking trail perfect for birdwatching (it's a stop on the Great Florida Birding Trail). And for breakfast, or after working up an appetite, **dig into pancakes cooked on tableside griddles** at The Old Spanish Sugar Mill restaurant, located in the park.

Grocery Stores

Grocery Stores

- **Publix Super Market**
  Regency Village Shopping Center
  8145 Vineland Ave
  Orlando, FL 32821
  (407) 238-9924
  (Near Tuscany Village & Oasis Lakes)

- **Lake Buena Vista Supermarket**
  13400 S Apopka Vineland Rd
  Orlando, FL 32821
  (407) 938-9260
  (Near Grand Beach & Sheraton Vistana)

- **Walmart Supercenter**
  3250 Vineland Rd
  Kissimmee, FL 34746
  (407) 397-1125

Grocery Stores

- **Publix Super Market**
  Williamsburg Town Center
  5350 Central Florida Pkwy
  Orlando, FL 32821
  (407) 239-0844
  (Near Marriott's Grande Vista)

- **Costco**
  Orlando Business Center
  2101 Waterbridge Blvd
  Orlando, FL 32837-9283

- **Trader Joe's**
  8323 Sand Lake Rd
  Orlando, FL 32819
  (407) 345-0611

Restaurants

> Orlando

Restaurants

- **PioPio**
  - Packed during lunchtime, where locals drive from everywhere during their lunch break to eat a good home-cooked meal.
  - 2500 South Semoran Blvd., Orlando, FL 32822 (407) 207-2262 or (321) 947-614
  - http://piopios.com/
- **Yellow Dog Eats Cafe**
  - Located in Windermere, this gem of a place really unique and funky. The place is famous with the locals for its awesome sandwiches.
  - 1236 Hempel Ave Windermere, FL 34786
  - (407) 296-0609
  - http://yellowdogeats.com/
- **Amura**
  - Fresh sushi and great steaks with an extensive wine list to complement your dinner. This place was voted the best sushi place in Orlando.
  - Plaza Venezia, 7786 W Sand Lake Rd, Orlando, FL
  - (407) 370-0007
  - http://amura.com/

Restaurants

- **Pho Vinh**
  - A large menu of Vietnamese dishes to suit any taste and any budget
  - 657 N. Primrose Dr., Orlando, Fl 32803
  - Tel: 407-228-0043
  - http://www.phovinhorlando.com/
- **Tibby's New Orleans Kitchen**
  - Tibby's is not just about what you see, but how it makes you feel. It's about expressing personality and character through food, music, art and heritage
  - 2203 Aloma Ave. Winter Park
  - 407-672-5753
- **Dexter's**
  - Can't decide on a bar or restaurant date? Dexter's is both. Decision made. The kitchen takes notable dishes does them just a little bit better. The applewood bacon-wrapped filet mignon and orange wood grilled salmon with leek and pancetta corn cream are winners. And the brunch is one of the most affordable in Central Florida.
  - 808 E. Washington St.
  - 407-648-2777

Appendix L

Restaurants

Restaurants

- **Graffiti Junktion American Burger Bar**
  - Burgers are king at Graffiti Junktion. They were expertly cooked, and the buns were ultra-fresh. Chicken wings here are another bargain
  - 900 E. Washington St., Thornton Park, Orlando
  - 407-426-9503
- Q'Kenan
  - Latin cuisine
  - 8117 Vineland Ave, Orlando, FL 32821
  - Phone number (407) 238-0014
- Bite30
  - Bite30 is Orlando's 30-Day Restaurant Week, featuring the best local restaurants and chefs driving Orlando's culinary scene
  - From June 1 to 30, participating restaurants offer special prix fixe menus that offer multicourse lunches or dinners at a set price ($15 for lunch, $30 for dinner)

Restaurants

- Conquer your impatience and enjoy a **Lineage** pour-over, handcrafted from beans painstakingly sourced, micro-roasted and ground by one of the guys brewing your cup (Lineage at East End Market, 3201 Corrine Drive, **lineageroasting.com**).
- Try a Cuban sandwich at one of Orlando's many Cuban eateries. A couple of our faves include **Cuban Sandwiches to Go** (1605 Lee Road) and **ZaZa New Cuban Diner** (3500 Curry Ford Road; **zazacubandiner.com**).

Gospel/Musical Brunch

Orlando

- ***Bananas Gospel Brunch***
  924 N. Mills Ave.
  Orlando, FL 32803
  P: 407.480.2200
  10 a.m. – 2 p.m., **$12.95**
  http://bananasdiner.com/bananas.html

- **Kirk Franklin's Gospel Brunch**
  House of Blues Orlando
  1490 E. Buena Vista Dr.
  P.O. Box 22804
  Lake Buena Vista, FL 32830
  (407) 934–BLUE (2583)
  10:30 a.m. and 1:00 p.m.
  $22.25 – Child (3–9), **$40.50 – Adult (10+)**
  http://www.houseofblues.com/venues/clubvenues/orlando/gospelbrunch.php

- **Rollicking Raglan Road Sunday Brunch**
  1640 Buena Vista Drive
  Lake Buena Vista, Florida 32836
  (407) 938-0300 11 a.m. – 4 p.m. **$8 to $26**
  http://www.raglanroad.com/the-rollicking-raglan-sunday-brunch

- **Sunday Gospel Brunch at House of Blues Orlando**
  (1490 E. Buena Vista Drive, Lake Buena Vista; **houseofblues.com**). $41.50 at 10:30 a.m. and 1 p.m.

Shopping (Outlet Malls, etc.)

- Renninger's Flea and Farmer's Market in Mount Dora is home to hundreds of dealers that sell just about anything you could imagine. Shoppers can find products from fresh produce, clothing, crafts, fresh meats, pets and pet supplies, foliage, collectibles, jewelry, and a whole lot more. In addition to our air-conditioned, indoor building (housing over 100 booths), our outdoor pavilions house over 400 spaces, and you can find even more dealers in our open-air spaces! If you've been searching for a place to browse and shop high-quality antiques and collectibles, look no further. In our 40,000-square-foot, air-conditioned building, you'll find over 180 antique booths staffed by their friendly and helpful owners. Outside of the indoor antique center, you will find the Street of Shops. A series of small buildings line paths and walkways full of wonderful antiques and merchandise.
- Buy a $4 suit – seriously – at **Community Thrift** (5456 S. Orange Ave.).
- I-drive 360: Orlando's newest entertainment destination! Home of the 400-foot "Orlando Eye" featuring attractions, restaurants, live entertainment and shopping. Conveniently located on International Drive with free parking.

Shopping (Outlet Malls, etc.)

Orlando

- **Orlando Premium Outlets®**
  8200 Vineland Avenue
  Orlando, FL 32821
  (407) 238-7787
  http://www.premiumoutlets.com/outlets/outlet.asp?id=17

- **Orlando Premium Outlets®**
  4951 International Drive
  Orlando, FL 32819
  (407) 352-9600
  http://www.premiumoutlets.com/outlets/outlet.asp?id=96

- **Lake Buena Vista Factory Stores**
  15657 South Apopka Vineland Road
  Orlando, FL 32821
  (407) 238-9301
  lbvfs.com

- **Outlet Marketplace**
  5269 International Drive
  Orlando, FL 32819
  (407) 352-9600
  http://www.premiumoutlets.com/outlets/outlet.asp?id=94

- **St. John Outlet**
  4953 International Drive
  Suite 1A-01
  Orlando, FL 32819
  (407) 352-5646
  http://www.discoverstjohn.com/

Shopping (Outlet Malls, etc.)

- **Artegon Marketplace**
  5250 International Drive
  Orlando, FL 32819
  (407) 351-7718
  http://www.artegonmarketplace.com/

Nightlife Venues

Orlando

- See a show at the **Dr. Phillips Center for the Performing Arts** (445 S. Magnolia Ave., **drphillipscenter.org**), downtown Orlando's new centerpiece. The venue itself is impressive – all modern, sleek interiors and pleasing acoustics – but really it's the excellent programming that's making the splash.
- Universal CityWalk
  - ▲▲ 6000 Universal Blvd, Orlando, FL 32819
  - ▲▲ This is where it all comes together. This is where unforgettable family fun meets restaurants that don't just make you say "Yum," but "Wow." The one place where the dining tastes of every member of the family and entertainment everyone can enjoy all intersect. It's everything you're looking for. And anything but ordinary. Universal CityWalk
  - ▲ https://www.universalorlando.com/Nightlife/Citywalk-Nightlife.aspx
- Church Street Station
  - ▲▲ Orlando's Church Street District
  - ▲▲ Church Street Station is downtown Orlando's new dining and nightlife epicenter located in the heart of the historic Church Street District. With more than 30 venues, the Station features world-class restaurants, exciting clubs, plush bars and a thriving after-hours scene for all ages.
  - ▲ http://visitchurchstreet.com/nightlife.html

Nightlife Venues

- **The Hoop-Dee-Doo Revue**
  - Vaudeville-style entertainment at an all-you-can-eat buffet.
- **Mama's Comedy Show**
  - Like Whose Line Is It Anyway for Adults! This is a Comedy Show for grown-ups
- **Treasure Tavern**
  - If you are looking for a night out of quality entertainment and great food, you should check out this new show in Orlando.
- **Ghost tours**
  - There are scary places all over Florida, and the Orlando area is no exception
- **Medieval Times**
  - Watch knights battle it out jousting style while you eat with your hands.
- **Wonder Works Comedy Magic Dinner Show**
  - At night they do an improv comedy and magic routine that is family-friendly. The menu is a highly sophisticated offering of all-you-can-eat pizza, salad, popcorn and dessert with a side of beer and pop.
- **Church Street Station Complex**
  - It is a lively night spot with bars and shops. There is an entrance fee into the complex but lots to see in there.
- **Menealo Martes – Shake it Tuesdays Latin Industry Night**
  - House of Blues
  - 1490 East Buena Vista Drive, Lake Buena Vista, FL 32830
  - **Time:** 10:30 p.m.
  - **Admission:** Free for service industry employees 21+, $8 for non-service industry 21+

Nightlife Venues

Orlando

- **Atlantic Dance Hall**
  - 2101 N Epcot Resort Blvd, Lake Buena Vista, FL
  - (407) 824-2222
- **3Nine**
  - 9700 International Dr, Orlando, FL 32819
  - Phone number (407) 996-9700
- **Icebar Orlando**
  - 8967 International Dr, Orlando, FL 32819
  - Phone number (407) 426-7555
- **Cuba Libre Restaurant & Rum Bar**
  - 9101 International Dr, Orlando, FL 32819
  - Phone number (407) 226-1600
- **Mango's Tropical Café**
  - 8126 International Dr, Orlando, FL 32819
  - Phone number (407) 673-4422
- **Kings Orlando**
  - 8255 South International Drive, Suite 120
  - Orlando, FL 32819
  - 407-363-0200
- **Tin Roof**
  - 8371 International Drive Suite 100, Orlando, FL
  - 407-270-7926

Appendix L

Entertainment & Nightlife

I-Drive 360

- 360 Degrees of Nonstop Fun. Welcome to I-Drive 360, Orlando's new $250 million attraction and entertainment destination and home to The Coca-Cola Orlando Eye. Located in the heart of Orlando's popular International Drive, the Orlando Eye's 400-foot iconic observation wheel is the centerpiece of this metro-chic-themed complex featuring a dynamic blend of attractions, restaurants, clubs and shops. Joining the Coca-Cola Orlando Eye as part of I-Drive 360's unique lineup of attractions are world-famous Madame Tussaud's, SEA LIFE Aquarium and Skeletons: Animals Unveiled!. These attractions offer guests great entertainment with maximum flexibility, complementing Orlando's legendary full-day theme parks. An equally unique lineup of restaurants features a variety of flavorful experiences and dining options, from full service to fast casual and quick serve. Popular brand restaurants, including Outback Steakhouse, Carrabbas' Italian Grill, Yard House, Buffalo Wild Wings and Shake Shack, are joined by unique establishments such as Tapa Toro, Naru, Paramount Fine Foods and Sugar Factory. High energy entertainment is on tap at Tin Roof and Cowgirls Rockbar, featuring Orlando's only mechanical bull. Visitors looking to chill out following an intense day of shopping or theme-park hopping can park for free in I-Drive 360's massive seven-story covered parking structure and in minutes find themselves sitting in an open-air courtyard featuring a $1.5-million-dollar water show set to music and color-changing lights, enjoying their favorite refreshment. Fun, variety, fun, dining, fun, entertainment, fun, flexible, fun, convenient. Did we say we were fun?!

Games/Contests

Orlando

- **Wii Game – Monday**
  - Bowling
- **Name Search Game – Tuesday**
- **Family Feud Game**
- **Card Game – Wednesday**
  - Spades
- **Game Show – Thursday**
  - Include questions from family history briefings
- **Bonus Guessing Jar – Guess due Thursday**

Games/Contests Prizes

- Wii Game – Holding Hand Crosses
- Family Members Name Search Game – N/A
- Family Feud Game – Just Certificates
- Card Game – Two-Sided Deluxe Note Caddy & Bound Note pads
- Game Show – Jazz Music Lover Tapestry
- Bonus Guessing Jar – Jar full of items
- Grand Prize – Core Crystal Award trophy and one week in one-bedroom timeshare

Jars

Spare Jar from Last Reunion
(13" H x 6" W x 4" D)

The Family Reunion Bible

Orlando

Appendix L

Grand Prize Trophy

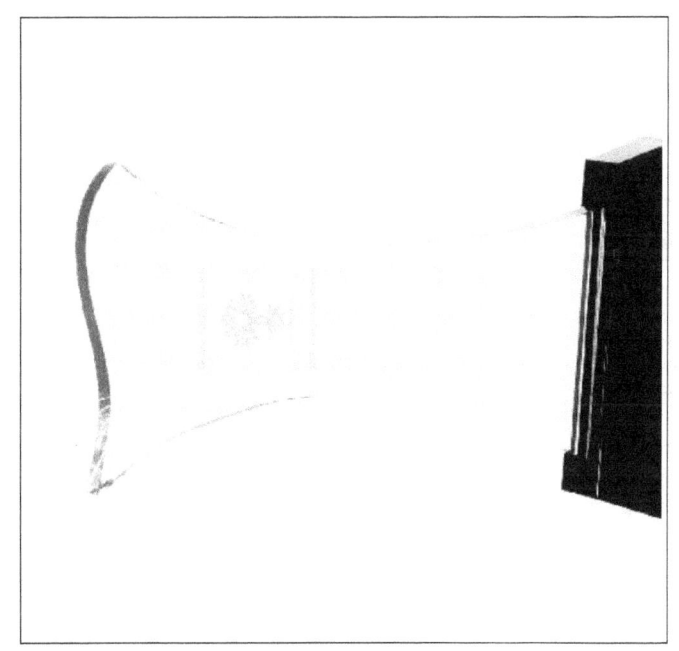

FRONT

The Family Reunion Bible

Orlando

Previous Game Winners

Appendix L

Optional Activities
Churches

- **Peace United Methodist Church**
  13502 Town Loop Blvd
  Orlando, FL 32837
  (407) 438-8947
  8:15 a.m. – Traditional Early Acoustic Service
  9:30 a.m. – Contemporary Worship Service With Praise Team
  11:00 a.m. – Traditional Service With Chancel Choir
  http://www.peaceumcorlando.org/

- **The Rock Church**
  5515 W Irlo Bronson Memorial Hwy
  Kissimmee, FL 34746
  (407) 396-7777
  The Rock Churches are a family of nondenominational churches reaching across all seven continents.
  8:00 a.m. – West Wing
  11:00 a.m. – Arena
  https://therockchurches.com/

- **Central Parkway Baptist Church**
  5281 Central Florida Parkway
  Orlando, FL 32821
  (407) 352-8664
  8:30 a.m., 11:00 a.m. – Worship
  http://cpbcorlando.com/

235

The Family Reunion Bible

Commute Time to Churches

Orlando

Resort	Peace United Methodist	The Rock	Central Parkway Baptist
HGVC Tuscany Village	11 mins	11 mins	9 mins
Grand Beach	12 mins	8 mins	15 mins
Marriott's Grande Vista	16 mins	18 mins	7 mins
Oasis Lakes at The Fountains	16 mins	14 mins	9 mins
Sheraton Vistana	16 mins	14 mins	9 mins

Optional Activities

Parks

- ### Dr. P. Phillips Community Park
  Sizable lakeside park with classic and wet playgrounds plus sports fields, picnic areas and a dog run.
  Address: 8249 Buena Vista Woods Blvd, Orlando, FL 32836
- ### Lake Eola
  One of the most popular lakes in Orlando. This lake is located in the heart of downtown Orlando and hosts multiple events. The annual Downtown Food and Wine Festival is held in this park, as well as a farmer's market every Sunday. Lake Eola also offers swan-shaped paddleboat rides (sidenote: last time I checked, there was a discount for paddleboat rentals on Groupon), and there is a 0.9-mile walking trail surrounding it. I would recommend having a picnic during sunset, the view is incredible.

The Family Reunion Bible

Orlando

Friday Night Buffet Dinner Options

- **Golden Corral**: 8707 Vineland Avenue, Orlando, FL 32821 (Also: 8032 International Drive) **$12**
- **Hibachi Buffet**: 6107 S Orange Blossom Trail, Orlando, FL 32809 – **$8.99, Child (3–8 yrs): $4.99**
- **Gilson's Brazilian Restaurant**
  8191 Vineland Ave, Orlando, FL 32821
  (407) 787-3494
  Gilson's is a Brazilian fine dining buffet-style restaurant. Go to the buffet and pick from a large variety of Brazilian traditional foods, as rice, black beans, filet mignon, vegetables, dry meats, cheese, the famous Brazilian cheese bread, pastas, desserts, and on and on. Free shuttle offered! Call (407) 352-1255 and we will be pleased to bring you!
  Adult $25.99, **Kids $ 13.99**
  http://gilsonsrestaurant.com/
- **Ichiban Japanese Buffet**: 5269 W Irlo Bronson Memorial Hwy, Kissimmee, FL 34746 (or 5529 International Dr, Orlando, FL)
  An upscale Asian fusion restaurant, Ichiban Buffet features all-you-can-eat sushi, hibachi grill, Asian dishes. Signature dinner entrees include delicious lobsters and crab legs.
  Adult $11.99, Adult (with crab legs) $16.99, **Kids (age 4–11 & 3–5 ft.) $7.99**
  http://www.ichibanbuffet.com/home.html
- **Tusker House:** The "wide variety" of "flavorful" African and American dishes at this "huge" all-day buffet in Disney's Animal Kingdom manages to "please all palates" while giving kids the chance "to meet Mickey Mouse" in a rustic, "colonial" setting. Adult – $44.72, Child – $26.62
  https://disneyworld.disney.go.com/dining/animal-kingdom/tusker-house-restaurant/

Friday Night Buffet Dinner Options (continued)

- Panda Express: 7653 International Dr, Orlando, FL – Adults: $9.95, Child: 5.95 https://www.pandaexpress.com/
- Café Mineiro Brazilian Steakhouse: 6432 International Dr, Orlando, FL. Strives to be the premier family Brazilian steakhouse restaurant in the mid-price casual dining range – $30 (10 meats), $16 (4 meats) http://www.cafemineirosteakhouse.com/index.php/en/#specials
- Sinha Brazilian Steak House: 13586 Village Park Dr, Orlando, Fl 32837 Hot Buffet and Salad: Adults – $12.90, Child (6–10 yrs) – $6.45 Brazilian Rodizio of meats: Adults – $19.90, Child (6–10 yrs) – $8.95 (includes hot buffet and salads plus Brazilian meats: pork sausages, flank steak, top sirloin with garlic, top sirloin, sirloin with bacon, chicken heart, sirloin, garlic bread http://www.sinhabraziliansteakhouse.com/

Other Activities/Items

Orlando

- T-shirts
- Family pot luck dinner
  – Tuesday
- Display table showing previous items
- Projector
- Projector screen
- Portable printer
- Laser pointer to use with presentations.

Appendix L

Discussions, Ideas, etc. for Next Reunion
(Friday after Buffet)

- Do we want to collect money for common expenses?
  - Souvenirs, etc.
  - People should pay with their tax refunds from the year before the family reunion
  - Family reunion dues – money now?
  - Treasurer – Alma?
  - Fundraiser?
- 2019 reunion location options
  - Sarasota, FL
  - Daytona Beach, FL
  - Fort Lauderdale, FL
  - Panama City/Destin, FL
  - Hilton Head, SC
  - Tampa/St. Pete, FL
  - Myrtle Beach, SC
  - Smoky Mountains
  - New Orleans
- Ways to open lines of communication with other family members
- Send out newsletter on future locations and heads up on 2017 reunion
  - Highlights from previous reunions (prize winners, activities, # attendees, etc.
  - Pictures
  - Summary of this reunion
  - Include family website link.
  - Snail mail, email, etc.
  - Other items?
- Can some people make monthly payments toward their cost?
  - Layaway plan
  - Survey to find out why people do not attend.
- Explain the importance of having this reunion

The Family Reunion Bible

Orlando

Income & Expenses

- Insert spreadsheet

Appendix L

Puerto Vallarta Vacation Reference Charts

Appendix L

The Family Reunion Bible

Mexico

Topics

- Welcome & Kickoff Prayer
- Theme
- Family Descriptions
- Awards
- People Locations
- Resort Map
- Unit Comparison
- Games/Contests
- Previous Game Winners
- Family Group Activities
- Money
- Getting Around
- Parking In Town
- Guest Book

- Family Vacation Book(s)
- Safety
- Crime Areas In Mexico
- Kids Club
- Attractions/Activities
- Hidden Gems
- Tips
- Day Trips
- Tours
- Grocery Stores
- Restaurants
- Family Fiesta Potluck
- Shopping (Outlet Malls, etc.)
- Nightlife Venues

Welcome & Kickoff Prayer

> **Welcome to the Our Family Vacation!**

"Let us all rejoice together, oh family and friends, and praise God for this opportunity He has provided to us so that we could be together on this joyous vacation."

Prayer by the Reverend

Theme

> Mexico

- Fiesta!
    - Mexican food may have become part of mainstream culture and dining, but authentic Mexican traditions and festivities such as the fiesta are still a great source of creativity for family reunions
    - Family potluck fiesta
    - Wear something Mexican if have something
    - Pinata decorations
    - Fiesta decorations

How Members Describe Our Family

- Our family is Great
- Loving
- Committed to family
- Our family represents greatness
- Dedicated, hardworking, and travel-oriented
- Strong, spiritual
- Loving, caring, fun, real
- Friendly, caring and close-knit family.
- Loving, Christian, close-knit
- Our family is loving
- Resilient

The Family Reunion Bible

Mexico

Awards

- 2019 Awards
  - Who has the most children present?
  - Who has the most grandchildren present?
  - Who has the most gray hair *showing*?
  - Who never left school (became a teacher!)?
  - Most jobs since high school?
  - Least number of jobs since high school?
  - Random number prize
  - Most tattoos?
  - Who has worked the longest at one job?
  - Who has had the most operations?

Appendix L

People Locations
(Resort People Reside At)

- **Grand Luxxe**
  Paseo de Las Moras
  Nuevo Vallarta, Nay., Mexico
  +52 322 226 4000
  ➤ 4-Bed Unit #: _____
    - People

- **Grand Luxxe**
  Paseo de Las Moras
  Nuevo Vallarta, Nay., Mexico
  +52 322 226 4000
  ➤ 3-Bed Unit #: _____
    - People

The Family Reunion Bible

People Locations
(Resort People Reside At)

Mexico

- **Grand Luxxe**
  Paseo de Las Moras
  Nuevo Vallarta, Nay., Mexico
  +52 322 226 4000
  ➤ 2-Bed Unit #: _____
  - People

- **Grand Bliss**
  Paseo de Las Moras
  Nuevo Vallarta, Nay., Mexico
  +52 322 226 4000
  ➤ 2-Bed Unit #: _____
  - People

Resort Map

The Family Reunion Bible

Unit Comparison

Mexico

Grand Luxxe Nuevo Vallarta Unit Comparison

Bed-rooms	Unit Type (Retail Price/Night)	Building	Floors	Kids Club	Square Feet	Occupancy Adults	Occupancy < Age 12	Beds	Baths	Oven	# Kitchens	# Living Room	Washer/Dryer	Rooftop Pool	TVs	# Plunge Pools
2 Bed	Suite ($2,730/Night)	Tower 1	All	No	2,300	6	2	2K	2.5	No	1	1	No	No	3	1
		Tower 2	All	No												
		Tower 3	All but 3	Yes												
		Tower 4	1 - 3	No												
		Tower 5B	1 - 8	No										Yes		
2 Bed	Villa ($2,890/Night)	Tower 1	All	No	2,800	8	2	2K	2.5	No	1	2	No	No	4	1
		Tower 2	All	No												
		Tower 3	All but 3	Yes												
		Tower 4	1 - 3	No												
		Tower 5B	1 - 8	No										Yes		
	Presidential Villa ($3,020/Night)	Punta	All	No	2,700	6	2	1K + 2D	2.5	No	1	1	No	No	3	1
	Spa Suite ($3,060/Night)	Tower 4	4 - 9	Yes	2,300	6	2	2K	2.5	No	1	1	No	No	3	1
	Loft ($10,920/Night)	Tower 3	3	Yes	3,400	6	2	2K	2	Yes	1	2	Yes	No	4	1
		Tower 4	3	Yes												
		Tower 5B	9	No										Yes		
3 Bed	Presidential Villa ($3,740/Night)	Punta	All	No	4,246	10	2	2K + 2D	3.5	No	2	2	No	No	5	2
3 Bed	Spa Suite ($3,700/Night)	Tower 4	4 - 9	Yes	3,200	8	2	2K + 2Q	3	No	1	1	No	No	4	1
	Loft ($13,000/Night)	Tower 3	3	Yes	5,000	8	2	2K + 2D	3.5	Yes	1	2	Yes	No	5	1
		Tower 5B	9	No										Yes		
4 Bed	N/A ($14,840/Night)	Residence	All	No	6,000	12	2	2K + 4D	4.5	Yes	1	1	Yes	Yes	6	1

Appendix L

Unit Comparison

Grand Bliss Nuevo Vallarta Unit Comparison

Bed-rooms	Unit Type	Building	Floors	Kids Club	Square Feet	Occupancy Adults	Occupancy < Age 12	Beds	Baths	Oven	# Kitchens	# Living Room	Washer/Dryer	Rooftop Pool	TVs	# Plunge Pools
2 Bed	Master Suite	Grand Bliss	All	No	1,898	6	2	2K	2	No	1	1	No	No	3	1

Mexico

Games/Contests

- Wii Game – Prize*
- Random Number
- Bingo – Prize*
- Cactus Ring Toss – Prize*
- Bonus Guessing Jar – Jar full of items
- Grand Prize – Trophy*

*Prizes will be purchased in Mexico

Appendix L

Previous Game Winners

The Family Reunion Bible

Family Group Activities
(Locations)

| Mexico |

- Orientation
- Games
- Potluck dinner
- Leftover feast

Money

Payment Methods Accepted

1. Credit Cards
   - Best method to use if accepted
   - Use a card that doesn't have foreign exchange fees
2. US Dollars
   - You will get change in pesos
   - More costly since you will receive change using an unfavorable exchange rate
3. Pesos
   - Best option when credit cards are not an option
   - Don't accept any partially torn or taped-together notes
4. Traveler's Checks
   - Not widely used anymore
   - Exchange for pesos at a bank if you have them

The Family Reunion Bible

Mexico

Money (Continued)
Where to Exchange US Dollars for Pesos

1. **Airport**
   - Airport money exchanges are the most expensive option – Unfavorable exchange rates, fees (Airport bank ATM machines may be OK)

2. **ATM**
   - Use <u>debit</u> cards with no foreign exchange fees
   - Usually best rates if there are no exchange rate or ATM fees
   - If available, use ATMs associated with your bank for fewer fees

3. **Bank (Will need to show your passport)**
   - Compare exchange rates for various banks
   - Many banks display exchange rates up front
   - "The Dollar in Mexico" and other apps list exchange rates for all banks

4. **Casas de Cambio (Money Exchange)**
   - Compare exchange rates for various companies
   - Rates comparable to banks

5. **Resort**
   - Usually not a good rate

Money (Continued)

Mexican bills come in denominations of 20, 50, 100, 200, 500 and the very rare 1000 pesos.
Mexican coins comes in denominations of 1, 2, 5, 10 and the rare 20 Pesos.
Mexico Centavos (cents) are 5, 10, 20 and 50 (**100 centavos = 1 peso**).

General Tipping Guide [In Pesos (MXN)]	
Tip Description	**Pesos**
Aiport Porter bag help to shuttle (per bag)	20
Airport shuttle help with luggage (per bag)	$10
Taxi/uber driver help with luggage/groceries (per bag)	$10
Bellhop (bringing luggage to room)	$30
Bellhop (bringing groceries to room)	$40
Day Maid (2 to 4 bedroom unit)	$40 to $60
Night Maid (2 to 4 bedroom)	$10 to $30
Grocery Baggers (taking bags to car)	$10
Grocery Baggers (per transaction)	$15
Restaurant Servers	10 - 20%
Bartender	10 - 15%
Tour Guide Operator	10 - 20%
Spas	15%
Gas Station Attendant	$15
Bathroom Attendant	$5
Musicians	$10

Appendix L

Getting Around

Mexico

Bus

- The bus stop is by the Sea Garden across from the Oxxo. There are two busses that go to PV, the directo, which goes straight there, or the Riu, which goes north along the coast as far as the Riu and the Villa Del Palmar Pelicanos just south of Bucerias before heading south on the highway to PV. Both go just a bit past the Buganvilias Resort to the bus terminal, which is a 15–20 minute walk to the Malecon. On the way back, the Riu bus stops in NV before circling back up north, so it doesn't really matter which bus you catch. Cost is 18 pesos each way. The local bus is 7.5 pesos.

Taxi

- Fares are charged by zone, not meter, so always agree on a fare before hopping in. The minimum fare is usually around 40 to 70 pesos ($2.10 to $3.70) around town, but rides from the airport to most hotels will likely start around the equivalent of $10 (1 to 3 people). They always seem to be short of change. Keep a stash of 10-peso coins and 20-peso notes for these trips.

Uber

- Cheaper than taxis. Taxi drivers have been known to have problems with them so don't request them around taxis if possible. The app works well in Puerto Vallarta.

Appendix L

Getting Around
(Bus)

ROUTE: From Nuevo Vallarta to downtown Puerto Vallarta (Centro/Malecon)

- Total bus fare for this one-way trip: $22.5 pesos.
- Take an ATM bus to Puerto Vallarta. Bus fare is $15 pesos.
- ATM buses arrive at bus stops in Nuevo Vallarta every 20–30 minutes.
- Get off the ATM bus in Puerto Vallarta once you reach the Maritime Terminal across the street from Walmart and Sam's Club.
- On that same side of the street (opposite Walmart) wait close to the intersection for a bus with *Centro* written on the windshield.
- Buses that indicate BOTH Centro and Tunel are heading to the Romantic Zone without stopping downtown.
- Bus fare from the Maritime Terminal to downtown Puerto Vallarta is $7.5 pesos.

Mexico

Getting Around
(Bus)

ROUTE: From downtown Puerto Vallarta (Romantic Zone) to Mismaloya, Vallarta Zoo & Boca de Tomatlan

- Bus fare is $8 pesos.
- Take an ORANGE & WHITE bus at the corner of Basilio Badillo and Constitution (by the OXXO convenience store).
- These orange & white buses only go as far as Boca de Tomatlan.
- These buses stop at Conchas Chinas, Dreams Resort, Presidente Intercontinental, Mismaloya, Boca de Tomatlan.

Appendix L

Getting Around
(Bus)

ROUTE: From downtown Puerto Vallarta (Romantic Zone) to the Botanical Gardens and El Tuito

- Bus fare is $20 pesos.
- Take a BLUE bus at the corner of V. Carranza and Aguacate.
- The windshield of the bus should state: *El Tuito / **Botanical Gardens***
- Buses come by every 20–30 minutes.
- It will take approximately 50 minutes to get to El Tuito.

The Family Reunion Bible

Getting Around
(Bus)

Mexico

ROUTE: From downtown Puerto Vallarta to Nuevo Vallarta

- Total bus fare for this one-way trip: $22.5 pesos.
- From the Malecon head east, walking a couple blocks up until you see a series of public buses zooming by.
- Look for a blue sign indicating a bus stop.
- Take any bus heading north that has *Walmart* written on the windshield. The bus fare is $7.5 pesos.
- Get off at Walmart. You'll notice two bus waiting areas. Facing Walmart and Sam's Club, walk to the larger bus waiting area on the left.
- There is usually a man with a clipboard stationed there to direct passengers to the correct bus for their desired destination.

(Continued on next page)

Appendix L

Getting Around
(Bus)

ROUTE: From downtown Puerto Vallarta to Nuevo Vallarta (Continued)

- Board an ATM bus that says *Nuevo Vallarta* (for southern NV) OR ***Riu*** for locations in Flamingos (northern NV). The Flamingos section of NV includes Villa la Estancia on the northern end and down to the Peninsula condo complex at the southern end of the neighborhood. For a good visual refer to the map of Nuevo Vallarta.

- If you're heading to the Flamingos area, it's important to know that the bus indicating "Nuevo Vallarta" does NOT service the "Flamingos" section of the neighborhood. To get to resorts and condos in Flamingos you MUST take a bus indicating "Riu" on its front windshield.

- The bus fare is $15 pesos.

- The last buses available to Nuevo Vallarta / Flamingos leave by 9 p.m.

Getting Around
(Bus)

> Mexico

- **HELPFUL SPANISH WORDS – BUS TRAVEL**
  - Bus: Autobus
  - Driver: Chofer
  - Passenger: Passajero
  - Schedule: Horario
  - Route: Ruta
  - Fare: Tarifa
  - Seat: Asiento
  - Destination: Destino
  - How long does it take to get to _____? Cuanto se demora en llegar a _____?

Parking in Town (PV)

Parking Garages

- **Parque Hidalgo**: At the north end of the Malecon there is paid underground parking below Hidalgo Park. Driving southbound on Ave. Mexico, the entrance is right after crossing Venezuela Street.
- **Parque Lazaro Cardenas**: In the Romantic Zone (South Side) there is a paid underground parking structure beneath Lazaro Cardenas Park on L. Cardenas and Pino Suarez. This underground parking lot may not be lit.
- **Benito Juarez**: At the south end of the Malecon just north of the Ignacio Vallarta Bridge (or just north of the Rio Cuale along the Malecon and Calle Rodriguez) there is a parking structure within the Benito Juarez Building.

Guest Book

Mexico

- Guest book is available for attendees to sign
  - Name
  - Home address
  - Email address
- The books from each reunion will be available for review at future reunions.
- Bring last year's book
- Alma to find book for this reunion to input sheets in

Family Vacation Book(s)

- Memento book will be published after the vacation
  - Step guidelines on planning and implementing a family (or other) reunion
  - Bound hardcover, softcover and e-book formats
  - Details from current reunion
  - Highlights from previous reunions
  - Will be available for purchase
    - Price to be determined once cost of production is known
    - Will be available on Amazon.com
    - Will need signed releases from everyone whose picture is shown

Safety

- The crime rates in Puerto Vallarta are very low, significantly lower than those of major cities in the United States like Miami, Las Vegas, and New Orleans. Violent crime is something that any visitor using common sense shouldn't encounter (As long as you don't get involved in the drug trade!)
- The United States Department of State has issued an updated travel advisory for Mexico, but all of the areas popular with tourists have still been deemed safe.
- General Safety Tips:
  - Don't make your electronics obvious
  - Daylight is on your side
  - Stay on the beaten path
  - Don't get too drunk
  - Learn the essentials of the language

Appendix L

Crime Areas in Mexico

Mexico

Kid's Club

Kid's Club: This fun-filled play facility offers an assortment of amazing activities, including water activities at the on premise pool, arts and crafts, games, and so much more. And every single activity is supervised by expert staff who are standing by to make your child's stay their best vacation ever!

➢ Details

Cost: $350 pesos for a full day, includes lunch from kids' menu

Half day: $200 pesos from 9:30 a.m. to 1 p.m. or 1:30 p.m. to 4:30 p.m.

Hours: Monday–Sunday, 9:30 a.m. to 4:30 p.m.

Ages: 5–12 years

Kid's Club Theme Nights: Weekly theme nights where you can drop off your children and enjoy an evening at the resort while they make new friends and try new things at events like Disco Night, Pirate Night, or a Pajama Party. There is also a Grand Luxxe-exclusive Kid's Club by Grand Luxxe Tower 4.

➢ Details

Cost: $350 pesos (7 p.m. – 10 p.m.)

Ages: 5–12 years (Includes dinner from the kids' menu)

Attractions/Activities

- **Los Arcos and El Malecon**: Stretching for more than a mile along Bahía de Banderas (Banderas Bay), *El Malecón* is a great place to stroll any time of day, but especially in the evenings. Along the way, visitors will see everything from sand sculptures and bronze sculptures to the iconic Church of Our Lady of Guadalupe.
- **Zona Romanitca**: This charming south side neighborhood is like a detached, unpretentious beach village that serves PV's more laid-back and less resort-conscious tourists. It's also the center of the city's strong gay population and has a bevy of gay beaches, bars and restaurants lining Olas Atlas. Travelers should keep in mind that this area is also known as Old Vallarta or Old Town.
- **Bucerias:** great place to experience the joys of a resort town without the tourist-palooza that is Puerto Vallarta, the small fishing village of Bucerías is steadily becoming a popular day trip for PV vacationers. If you have the time to spare, take a bus to this beach hideaway up the coastline for an afternoon of fishing or swimming.
Recent visitors recommend spending Thursday evenings doing the Bucerías Art Walk, a self-guided tour of more than a dozen galleries and art boutiques.
- **Playa Los Muertos:** The most popular shoreline in Puerto Vallarta, *Playa los Muertos* (Dead Man's Beach) in the Zona Romantica, offers opportunities to Jet Ski, windsurf and even parasail and an assortment of excellent restaurants and bars.

Mexico

Attractions/Activities

- **Isla Rio Cuale**: Isla Río Cuale is almost in the heart of the city and is actually an island set on an inlet of the Banderas Bay. To see the island, simply walk south from El Malecon until you reach a bridge that spans the river, and you'll discover the island.
- **Playa Las Gemelas**: A small shoreline located amid condo and beach rentals. Located about 10 miles south of central Puerto Vallarta, its cerulean waves and sandy shore are a nice place to break away from some of PV's more crowded beaches.
- **Church of Our Lady of Guadalupe**: The silhouette of this church in downtown PV is one of the most definable images of the resort town and its chiming church bells are one of the most recognizable sounds. Recent visitors said that you can enjoy visiting this parish by just pausing a moment during a Malecón stroll to admire the church's Renaissance-style tower. Others recommended stopping inside to see the gorgeous interior or attending Mass (English services are held Saturdays at 5 p.m. – a bilingual service is held every Sunday at 10 a.m.).
- **Biblioteca Los Mangos**: Library established more than 20 years ago as an educational epicenter for PV residents, can offer a neat break from playing tourist. It has a Cine Club, which screens a variety of artsy movies throughout each month, and they host various speakers on myriad cultural topics (granted, primarily in Spanish). Check out their online calendar of events when you're planning your stay. The library also houses more than 30,000 books, in both Spanish and English.

Attractions/Activities

- **El Salado Estuary:** A 418-acre urban sanctuary, and it's right in the heart of Puerto Vallarta's hotel zone. The estuary is home to over 100 species of birds, fish, fiddler and mouthless crabs. It's also home to dozens of species of amphibians and reptiles, including iguanas and crocodiles, which can often be spotted hiding out in the mangrove forests.

- **The Marina**: If you are looking for the perfect excuse to take a bus, but aren't sure where to, consider getting on a blue bus that has the words "Plz Marina" and head to the (you guessed it), Plaza Marina. Only a 10–15-minute bus ride from downtown, the marina is a great place to walk around, check out a good restaurant scene and enjoy looking at all the fancy, schmancy boats.

- **Vallarta Botanical Gardens:** The gardens feature an assortment of wildflowers and insect life that provides a relaxing and romantic getaway from the day-to-day hustle of Vallarta's downtown. You can also boulder the jungle's rocks and swim a section of the river. The gardens are generally open daily from 9 a.m. to 6 p.m., though hours can vary depending on the season. Keep in mind: The gardens are closed on Mondays during the months of April through November. The gardens are located just about 20 miles south of the city and accessible by taxi or the special "El Tuito" bus from the corner of Carranza and Aguacate in the Romantic Zone. Bus fare is 30 pesos (about $1.60) each way; buses leave every 30 minutes. Most past travelers arrived at the gardens via Uber. Admission to gardens costs 200 pesos (around $10.50) per adult.

The Family Reunion Bible

Attractions/Activities

Mexico

- **Tequila Tasting**: For a true tequila tasting experience, it would be ideal to travel straight to the source: Tequila, Jalisco. If you're not up for the 4+ hour drive, you've still got plenty of opportunities to taste tequila in Puerto Vallarta. A budget suggestion? Avoid the tours and visit one of the many tequila shops in town and along the Malecon. You'll get your fair share of samples and inevitably learn a thing or two about how the stuff is made from the chatty salesmen. It's also cheaper to buy a bottle here to last for all the happy hours of your trip instead of racking up a tab at the bar.
- **Self-guided Food Tour**: Sure, you can pay upward of $60 CAD for an English guide to take you around to some of the local restaurants in town. But a budget traveler wouldn't. Brush up on your Spanish and visit these places yourself. Wander the streets and follow your nose. Order something you've never heard of. Point at the food when you don't know what it's called. Have fun! We wrote an entire Mexican food guide here and think Puerto Vallarta is a great place to try foods outside of your comfort zone. Some of my favorite budget eats in the old town are the taco stands outside of the Guadalajara drugstore on Insurgentes, Cenaderia Celia on Lazaro Cardenas or any place that is busy (+ looks clean) and has a sign out front advertising 'Comida Corrida.'
- **Naval History Museum**: Hidden in plain sight at the main square near Los Arcos. Here you'll learn about the origins of the Navy in Mexico and the history of settlement in Puerto Vallarta. Entrance and tours are available and the museum is open Tuesday to Sunday. Admission is 45 pesos for adults and 30 pesos for students and seniors with valid ID.

Appendix L

Attractions/Activities

- **Emotions Casino:** It is in a modern complex and in a serene and secure environment that you will indulge in your favorite game. Find a variety of entertainment, including Blackjack and slot machines. A room is reserved for bingo and traditional sports bets are also available. The property offers a parking lot available at any time (located in the Galerias Vallarta mall).
- **Turtle Releases**: From roughly June to September each year, there are tons of turtle releases going on up and down the coast of Vallarta and it's not that tricky to stumble across one. One beach that does a ton of these releases is Playa Del Holi, so head down there at sunset and keep your eyes peeled for the baby turtle releases (**Vidanta has a turtle release program. Check at the resort for schedules**).

The Family Reunion Bible

Attractions/Activities
(Chosen by Family Members)

Mexico

- Relax and have some fun
- Visit a chocolate factory
- Shopping
- Go to the beach
- Sight see
- Spend time with family
- Eat some good street food
- Nap
- Get a massage
- Win some games
- Go on some excursions
- See a show
- Eat at a good resort restaurant
- Cultural experiences (historic sites and attractions
- Exercise
- Evening out somewhere
- Amusement/water park
- Video game
- Family day trip
- Music
- Resort night club
- Clubbing
- Golf
- Learning local dance
- Zip lining
- Games

Appendix L

Attractions/Activities

(Parts of past vacations you have enjoyed the most)

- All of them. Daytona Beach was very special
- Spending time with family, exploring the city and playing games
- Family game competitions, seeing everyone's competitive side come out
- Being with everyone in the same place/room and listening to stories and laughing
- Contests
- Seeing family we haven't seen in forever. Seeing a new place with new sites
- Games
- Family bonding, locations
- Family group activities, sightseeing, group meals

Hidden Gems

Mexico

- **Mismaloya:** Mismaloya may not be technically within city limits, but as the beach where Puerto Vallarta's destiny was permanently changed, it certainly warrants mention. Film buffs may recognize this still pristine playa from the classic movie Night of the Iguana.
- **Los Arcos Marine Park:** For visitors looking to enjoy a truly pristine slice of Puerto Vallarta, there is the paradise within paradise known as the Los Arcos Marine Park. Inaccessible by land, those wishing to experience its tropical confines must take a water taxi, which depart from the pier at Los Muertos Beach outside downtown Puerto Vallarta and transport passengers for less than $5.
- **The Church of our Lady of the Refuge:** Corner of Peru and Argentina, Puerto Vallarta.

Appendix L

Hidden Gems

- Mirador de La Cruz: https://www.puertovallarta.net/what_to_do/cerro-de-la-cruz-lookout

How to get to Mirador de la Cruz is rather simple if you know which street to take and can follow the signs. One of the best tips for hiking to Mirador de la Cruz is to start from the Malecon, making it a fairly straight path. From the Malecon, take Calle Abasolo away from the sea and head toward the towering hills behind the city. After a couple of blocks, you'll turn left on Calle Emilio Carranza and then take the first right onto Josefa Ortiz de Dominguez. Along the way, several hand-painted signs will point out how to get to Mirador de la Cruz. As you walk up the streets, you'll reach a long set of white stairs that leads to the overlook and the best view in Puerto Vallarta.

One of the simple tips for hiking to Mirador de la Cruz that will make it much easier is to take your time and snap some photos on the climb up the stairs. This will help you save your energy and give you plenty of stunning pictures to take home as memories. Other tips for hiking to Mirador de la Cruz are to bring some water and wear sturdy shoes since all the roads are uphill. However, the hike will only take you 15–20 minutes, so don't feel like you need to carry heavy bottles of water and snacks for along the way, making this one of the simplest free activities in Puerto Vallarta.

The Family Reunion Bible

Mexico

Hidden Gems

Cerro de La Cruz Lookout

Tips

- Never use outdated SPF. Sunscreens have a shelf life of 3–5 years. Look for an expiration date or see http://www.uspharmacist.com/index.asp for the shelf life of your brand.
- NEVER lose your FMT. It is your Visa and you need to turn it in when you depart at the airport. Keep it safe with your passport or other valuables.
- If you are staying in Bucerias or Nuevo Vallarta, the state is NAYARIT. If you are staying in Puerto Vallarta, the state is JALISCO. You will need this info when you fill out your FMT.

Day Trips

Mexico

- Jorullo Bridge: About twenty minutes outside of Puerto Vallarta, you'll find yourself on the Jorullo Bridge. It's 1,500 feet long and 500 feet above the Cuale River. What's cool about this is that it's the longest vehicle suspension bridge in the world! This is a new attraction in Puerto Vallarta, and it gives you the chance to enjoy an amazing view of the river and the Sierra Madre mountains from a high vantage point. You can also visit the crystal waters of El Salto waterfall and delight in the local food at Los Coapinoles restaurant. The Mexican eco-tourism company Canopy River is a good choice for this trip ($75, shuttle pickup from Nuevo Vallarta). http://canopyriver.com/en/activities/jorullo-bridge-hiking-tour

Day Trips

- Marieta Islands' Playa Escondida (Hidden Beach)
    - An hour off the coast of Puerto Vallarta

Day Trips

> Mexico

- Quimixto Waterfall
  - A 30-minute boat ride from the Puerto Vallarta marina (cost??)

Tours

Vallarta Eats Food Tours

Signature Taco Tour

Dive deeper into Mexican Culture and eat a wide variety of the everyday food that locals eat.

Departs daily at 10 a.m.

US$55 (includes ticketing and credit card processing fees)

Children under 12 are $39 and little ones under 4 are free!

Tacos After Dark

Tacos After Dark Tour is a great way to get the most out of your visit to Old Town Vallarta. After a day at the beach, enjoy a leisurely evening stroll around town sampling delicious Mexican street food.

Departs Sunday through Friday at 7 p.m.

US$55 (includes ticketing and credit card processing fees)

Tours

Mexico

- **Puerto Vallarta City Sightseeing**
  - Private sightseeing tour of Puerto Vallarta. Visit some of this resort town's most authentic and alluring attractions, including the beach that first put Puerto Vallarta on the map. Learn how tequila is made and enjoy a complimentary tasting. Includes the expertise of a knowledgeable guide. Set out with just your party and a personal guide/driver.
  - Private Van (**12 guests**) cost is $310 (**$25.83 per person if full**)
  - Sprinter Max (**19 guests**) cost is $460 (**$24.21 per person if full**)

- **Private City Tour**
  - Our city tour is perfect for both first-timers and regular visitors as we visit the traditional areas of Vallarta's downtown and old town. We will visit the main sights of Puerto Vallarta's main square, including the historical church, a traditional silver shop and tile factory with artisans on-site. We will take a short drive out to Mismaloya, remembered for being the setting for the famous movie "Night of the Iguana" with Richard Burton, stop at a local hacienda for a taste of Mexico's favorite drink, tequila, and take lunch at a riverside restaurant (optional). A very nice first look or overall view of Puerto Vallarta.
  - **Up to 10 People: $200** ($20 per person if full), **11 – 14 People: $250** ($17.86 if full)
  - **15 – 19 People: $375** ($19.74 if full)

*Even if the tours have deals for 15% off online or buy 2 get 1 free, we may be able to save more money buying them in PV. We will try to bargain down the tour. Also, only put a down payment until the day of the tour to make sure you don't get ripped off.

Tours

- **Chocolate Tour**
  - An exceptional tour through the garden where you will hear the narrative about the appreciation of cocoa, its symbolism and cultural uses, you will taste the fresh grains of the cocoa pod, taste a drink based on this generous seed and you will prepare your own handmade chocolate. Hours: 10:00 12:00 14:00 Reservations at 52 322 237 88 40 or planetacacao@gmail.com
  - About half an hour from Puerto Vallarta, in the small town of El Tondoroque – you'll find Planeta Cacao – a chocolate garden, founded by Laura Aguilar and Mina Ibira. Their mission is to share the cultural and symbolic importance of cacao, which has been grown in the area for over 1,000 years. But the history lesson is only part of why you'll want to come here.
  - $600 MXN (approximately $30 US).

The Family Reunion Bible

Mexico

Grocery Stores

Grocery Stores
(Nuevo Vallarta)

- La Plaza Grocery Store
  La Plaza
  Vidanta
  Nuevo Vallarta
- Sunset Market
  Paradise Village Shopping Center
  Nuevo Vallarta
- Sun Market
  Paseo de Las Moras
  Nuevo Vallarta

Grocery Stores
(Nuevo Vallarta)

- Sam's Club
  Carretera Federal 200
  Nuevo Vallarta
- Chedraul
  Golden Valley, Av Vale Dorado
  Nuevo Vallarta
- La Alacena
  Vidanta
  Nuevo Vallarta

Grocery Stores

Grocery Stores

(Best from resort or points North)

- Walmart Banderas Bay
  Tepic – Puerto Vallarta 430, Valle Dorado, 63732 San Vicente, Nay., Mexico
- La Comer Paseo Flamingos Lote 8–1, Flamingos Club Residencial, 63732 Nayarit, Nay., Mexico
- Mega Soriana
  Carretera Tepic-Vta Km 144 Nayarit Mexico

Grocery Stores

(Best for points South)

- Walmart
  Blvd Francisco Medina Ascencio 2900
- Soriana Super Playa de Oro
  Blvd Francisco Medina Ascencio 2735
- Mega Super (Mega Soriana)
  Av. Francisco Medina Ascencio 1800, Zona Hotelera Gloria
- Costco
  Avenida Fluvial Vallarta 134, Fraccionamiento Fluvial Vallarta

Mexico

Grocery Stores

How to Clean and Disinfect Fruits and Vegetables in Mexico

- Soil, microbes and bacteria are found on the skins of fruits and vegetables. Using an antibacterial product in a soak solution will ensure clean produce, whether it is to be eaten raw or cooked.
- Common products used in Mexico are **Microdyn** and **Bacdyn**. They are usually sold in grocery stores in the produce department
  - To soak: first wash off any obvious soil. Always read the instructions for the proportion of solution to water and how many minutes to soak. Various brands and different sizes of the same brand call for different amounts of concentration to water. Use tap water, not purified water, because the antibacterial product kills any bacteria in the water as well. After all, this is the same procedure for purifying unclean drinking water.
  - After soaking for the specified time, place produce in a colander or on a clean dish towel to drain. You don't need to rinse off the soak solution (unless you used chlorine bleach, and then only with pure water). Allow to air dry completely, as drier produce stays fresher longer in the fridge.

Appendix L

Vidanta Restaurants

Meal Plan (as of October 2018)

- Two different types of coupon books are available: Breakfast and Breakfast + Dinner
- 6 Breakfast Coupon Book*: $1935 MXN ($100.62 or $16.77 per meal)
- Food using coupon books can be shared except when dining at a buffet

*Regular cost for breakfast buffet is $19.24 for adults (lower prices for children 12 & under

Fine Dining

- Azur – This beautiful restaurant is the perfect place to explore the flavors of French cuisine
- Costa Arena – the fresh, ingredient-driven dishes of Californian cuisine with a gorgeous ocean view
- Epazote – The best of Mexican cuisine, elevated to stun the palate
- Gong – A tour of Asia's brightest flavors and favorite dishes
- Quinto Charcoal Grill – This rooftop eatery offers premium cuts, smoky flavors, and stunning views
- The Burger Custom Made – Gourmet burgers with a sophisticated twist
- Tramonto – A classic Italian trattoria combined with an American steak house
- 6 Breakfast and 6 Dinner Coupon Book: $5935 ($308.62 or $25.72 per meal)

Mexico

Vidanta Restaurants (Continued)

Casual Dining

- Aequa
- Ameca Social House
- Balance
- Balche
- Limon y Sal
- Café del Lago
- Chiringuito
- Fresh Co
- Havana Moon
- Il Forno di Gio
- La Cantina
- Mercado Mexico
- Ola Mulata
- Rummba
- Samba
- Si Snack
- Sweet Paris
- Sky Garden
- Tacos Break

Bar & Lounges

- Pools Bar
- Blue Nautique Bar
- Grand Vista Bar
- Library Bar
- Luxxe Bar
- The Grand Lobby Bar
- Santuario
- La Isla de Cocos

Restaurants (Nuevo Vallarta)

Cheap Eats $

- Tacos Break
  1 Boulevard De Nayarit
  Nuevo Vallarta
- 3x3 Authentic Food
  Paseo de los Cocoteros 8
  Nuevo Vallarta
- Santo Taco Taquereia
  Paseo de los Cocoteros 85 A Sur
  Paradise Plaza Local A-3
  Nuevo Vallarta
- Sabrosa Italia
  Valle Grande # 106
  Valle Dorado
  Nuevo Vallarta

Cheap Eats $

- La Isla Restaurant Bar
  Paseo de los Cocoteros 33
  Nuevo Vallarta
- Maringo
  Blvd Nuevo Vallarta 280-C
  Nuevo Vallarta
- Pancho's Takos
  Valle de Mexico # 113
  Colonia Valle Dorado
  Bahia de Banderas
  Nuevo Vallarta
- Mr. Pepperoni
  Boulevard Nuevo Vallarta
  esquina Av.
  Nuevo Vallarta

Appendix L 297

Restaurants (Puerto Vallarta)

Mexico

Restaurant

- Salud Super Food $
  Calle Olas Altas 534-A
  Zona Romantica
  Puerto Vallarta
- Bravos Restaurant Bar $$–$$$
  Calle Francisco
  Madero 263
  Col. Emiliand Zapata Old Town
  Puerto Vallarta
- Martini en fuego Grill Bar $$–$$$
  Francisco Madero 260
  Col. Emiliand Zapata
  Puerto Vallarta
- Siam Cocina Thai $$–$$$
  Calle Francisco i. Madero 271
  Colonio Emaillano Zapata
  Puerto Vallarta

Restaurant

- Merida Grill $$–$$$
  Calle Venustiano Carranza No.1 210
  Col Emiliano Zapata
  Puerto Vallarta
- Tuna Azul $$–$$$
  Francisca Rodriguez 155, altos
  Calle del Muelle de Puerto Vallarta
  Puerto Vallarta
- Lamara $
  Calle Hamburgo 108
  Puerto Vallarta
- Mariscos Cisneros $
  Calle Aguacate 271
  Col. E. Zapata
  Puerto Vallarta

Family Potluck Fiesta Sample Dinner Items

Dishes
- Pork carnitas
- Tacos
- Guacamole
- Red cabbage
- Salsa
- Tortilla bowls (filled with what you want)
- Brown rice with cilantro and lime

Drinks
- Tequila
- Margarita

Mexico

Shopping (Silver)

Silver Jewelry

- The shops on Olas Altas, the street 'behind' the beach
- The Malecon stores (and on Juarez) are not only more expensive but somewhat aggressive in their sales pitch
- Cassandran Shaw Jewelry on Basilio Badilio, two and a half blocks from the beach.
- Voted the beat jewelry store in Vallarta for the last 3 years
- Roberto's Silver. He is a legend with his fair prices and friendly personality

Shopping (Flea & Street Markets)

Flea & Street Market Saturday Market Co-Op
- Pulpito #127 (between Amapas and Olas Altas Streets, Puerto Vallarta, Mexico
- Every Saturday morning in the Romantic Zone of beautiful Puerto Vallarta, you can browse our farmer's market for freshly baked breads, quality organic vegetables, Sid's World Famous Chili, gorgeous flowers and some of the finest arts and crafts you will find in PV. Sit and relax in the shade while you enjoy a light breakfast of freshly baked pastries with coffee or tea. Or have a delicious lunch from one of our local chefs. Take home the best breads, fresh bagels, fabulous cheeses, pastries, pies and Chili Con Carne in town. • Every Saturday, year-round, from 9:00 a.m. to 1:00 p.m. It's a great way to spend a leisurely Saturday morning. Please LIKE us on Facebook at SaturdayMarketPV.

Shopping (Flea & Street Markets)

Mexico

Mercado Municipal
- Puerto Vallarta, Mexico
- Maze of shops that offers practically everything for tourists

Old Town Market Viejo Vallarta
- Puerto Vallarta

Flea Markets
- Between to two roads that cross the Cuale River, Puerto Vallarta, Mexico

Appendix L

Shopping (Shopping Malls)

Galerias (Galleria) Vallartas Shopping Mall
– Francisco Medina Ascencio Avenue No. 2920 Col. Education, Puerto Vallarta, MexicoMaze of shops that offers practically everything for tourists

Liverpool
– Avenida Francisco Medina Ascencio 2920 | Educacion, Puerto Vallarta 48338, Mexico

La Isla
– Puerto Vallarta Jalisco 2477 | Las Glorias, 48333, Puerto Vallarta 48343, Mexico

Paradise Plaza Shopping Center
– Av. Paseo de Los Cocoteros, Nuevo Vallarta, México

Shopping (Farmer's Markets)

Mexico

Three Hens and a Rooster
- Calle Francisco i. Madero # 280 | Inside the Lions Club, Puerto Vallarta
- Local Farmers and Artisans' Market in Old Town Puerto Vallarta. Every Saturday from 9 to 1, located inside The Lion's Club.

Riviera Farmers Market
- Paseo de los Cococteros | Centro Empresarial, Nuevo Vallarta 63735, Mexico

Nightlife Venues

Bar Oceano – Central/Malecon – 565 Paseo Diaz Ordaz, upstairs. Tel: 222-0959:

Mexican restaurant and cantina overlooking downtown and with one of the oldest (since 1955) and most famous local histories as Elizabeth Taylor, Richard Burton and Peter O'Toole used to drink and socialize there in the '60s and '70s. Serving Mexican, seafood and sandwiches, Bar Oceano is still popular. Sometimes with live jazz, mariachi and salsa music entertainment in the evenings. Daily, 8 a.m. – midnight.

Champions Sports Bar – Marina Vallarta – 435 Paseo de la Marina at Hotel Marriott:

Located in the Hotel Marriott Casa Magna and featuring two of the largest giant screens in town, nearly 5' by 8' and some 21 flat-screen televisions showing a multiple selection of programs. Serving tourist American foods such as burgers, sandwiches, pizza, appetizers and tacos until 1 a.m. and alcohol until closing. I have seen good reviews. Daily 11 a.m. – 2 a.m.

Chasers – Nuevo Vallarta – 570 Ave. Mexico at Blvd. de Nayarit. Tel: 297-7274

Sports bar and grill located just off of Highway 200 in front of El Tigre golf course, so a good place to meet friends after a round of golf. With NHL, NFL, NBA and other sporting games on six plasma TV screens. Under an open-air palapa, their food includes wings, ribs, pizza, burgers and fajitas. Daily, noon – 1 a.m.

Mexico

Nightlife Venues

El Faro Lighthouse Bar – Marina Vallarta – 245 Paseo de la Marina: El Faro lighthouse bar and cocktail lounge with guitar/easy listening music, open seating and panoramic views overlooks much of the marina from the 110-foot tower. Full bar and wine list, with general manager Gonzalo Martinez. El Faro is good for groups, welcomes walk-ins and is often crowded at sunset. Attire is casual; since 1988. Daily, 5 p.m. – 1 a.m.

La Vaquita – Downtown – 610 Paseo Diaz Ordaz:
The newest nightclub bar along the boardwalk Malecon. La Vaquita (the little cow) provides comfortable seating, chic decor and a live DJ that has been keeping them busy since opening in late December 2009. So now three of the best and hottest downtown Vallarta nightlife venues – Mandala, the Zoo, and La Vaquita – are lined right up next to each other on Diaz Ordaz street. The Cerveceria Union seafood and Mexican restaurant (where Las Palomas used to be) completes the lineup on that very loud and lively city block. Casual attire. Always 2 for 1 on Wednesdays. More photos and information. Daily, 7 p.m. – 6 a.m.

Nightlife Venues

Mandala – Central – 640 Paseo Diaz Ordaz:
Hip high-tech Puerto Vallarta club, restaurant & video bar, Mandala is next door to The Zoo and where Club 69/Mogambo used to be located (picture at left). Quite popular with the tourist and upscale crowds for its Hindu-style concept interior and the Spanish pop, electronic and party music selections. Has a Sky Bar lounge rooftop for drinks and the view. Mandala draws a large people-watching crowd on the Malecon too. Flashy, with formal dress; recommended. Locations also in Cancun, Los Cabos and Playa del Carmen. Cover often 100+ pesos. More photos and information. Daily, 6 p.m. – 6 a.m.

The Jazz Foundation – Downtown – 116 Allende, upstairs:
Newest hot spot with live music along the downtown boardwalk – a jazz club, bar and restaurant, with ocean views. Across the street from popular La Bodeguita del Medio. "A forum, a restaurant, a rest, a bar, class room, a stage, a window of life in the sea, where we worship the essence of life." Also occasional offerings of poetry, alternative tango, soul, R&B and funk. Check out more info on the Jazz Foundation where they include the food menu (soups, salad, main dishes) or at their Facebook page. Dancing, wireless Internet, pet friendly. Daily, 6 p.m. – 2 a.m.

Nightlife Venues

Zoo Bar – Central – 630 Paseo Diaz Ordaz:

Great sounds and a cool ambiance make the Zoo bar antro (photo left) one of the best nightclubbing and dance spots in Puerto Vallarta. The party music is a combination of techno, hip hop, dance, Latin, reggae and pop and the DJ at the Zoo night club knows how to mix 'em good. Nicely remodeled in March 2010: mixed reviews. Cover charge on weekends at around 100 pesos. Casual. Bar opens at noon with some light food; Music daily, 8 p.m. – 3 a.m. The Zoo – Paradise Village Mall, Nuevo Vallarta

If you're going downtown at night, the last bus leaves Nuevo Vallarta at 10:30 p.m., so make sure you go to the bus stop before then. You can ask at the front desk of your hotel as to where the bus stop is, they will let you know. Also, when the bus stops, don't be afraid to ask the bus driver if the bus goes to Walmart. I always asked just to be sure. When you're on the bus, you'll know when to get off because Walmart is huge, you can't miss it. Plus when you're on the bus you'll pass a sign that says Walmart one mile ahead. Like I said, once you get off the bus, you'll walk straight ahead about 3 blocks and you'll see another bus stop. It looks just like the bus stops in the US. You'll wait there until the "blue and white" bus comes that says "Centro" on the front of it. Centro means downtown in Spanish. Then you can take that bus all the way to the Malecon where the clubs start. The whole trip only costs 16.5 pesos. (12 to get to Walmart, and 4.5 to go downtown). I have to warn you though on the way back you'll have to take a taxi back to the resort, which will cost you $16 American dollars, because the buses do not run after 10:30 p.m.

BIBLIOGRAPHY

n.d. *8 Astonishing Family Mountain Vacations.* Accessed February 14, 2021. https://www.travelchannel.com/interests/family/photos/family-mountain-vacations.

99th Congress, 1st Session. 1985. "Family Reunion Month, 1985." In *United States Statutes at Large*, Volum 99, Citation 99, 2062 - 2063. Washington, DC: U.S. Government Printing Office.

n.d. *Best Summer Mountain Vacations For Families.* Accessed February 14, 2021. https://kidsareatrip.com/best-summer-mountain-vacations-for-families/.

Bible, New International Version. 2011. "Holy Bible." In *The Holy Bible, New International Version*, Mark 6: 30-32. Biblica (worldwide), Zondervan (US).

n.d. *Cambridge Dictionary.* https://dictionary.cambridge.org/us/dictionary/english/family.

center, Pew Research. 2010. *The Return of the Multi-Generational family Household.* March 18. http://www.pewsocialtrends.org/2010/03/18/the-return-of-the-multi-generational-family-household/.

Centers for Disease Control and Prevention. 2021. *COVID-19 and Cruise Ship Travel.* February 2. Accessed February 14, 2021. https://wwwnc.cdc.gov/travel/notices/covid-4/coronavirus-cruise-ship.

—. 2018. *Facts About Noroviruses on Cruise Ships.* October 15. Accessed February 14, 2021. https://www.cdc.gov/nceh/vsp/pub/norovirus/norovirus.htm.

Escape The Roomz. 2019. *USA's Best Escape Rooms.* March 31. Accessed March 31, 2021. https://escapetheroomz.com/top-100-us-escape-rooms-march-2019/.

Ganti, Akhilesh. 2020. *Investopedia.* August 3. Accessed December 24, 2020. https://www.investopedia.com/terms/b/budget.asp.

n.d. "Genesis." In *Holy Bible*.

Goran, Alison. 2009. *Best Resorts for Family Reunions.* July 31. Accessed March 27, 2021. https://www.travelandleisure.com/trip-ideas/family-vacations/best-resorts-for-family-reunions.

Grant, Lara. 2017. *The Best Hotels for Family Reunions in the U.S.* May 11. Accessed March 27, 2021. https://www.oyster.com/articles/the-best-hotels-for-family-reunions-in-the-u-s/.

group, epxedia. 2018. *Amrican vacation deprivation levels at a five-year high.* October 16. Accessed October 25, 2018. https://media.expediagroup.com/2018-10-16-American-vacation-deprivation-levels-at-a-five-year-high.

grouptravel.org. n.d. *Family reunion Statistics.* Accessed January 16, 2021. http://grouptravel.org/family-reunion/family-reunion-statistics/#:~:text=Over%2057%25%20of%20the%20family,group%20rates%20at%20hotels%20fast.

Hollinger, Nick. 2017. *Importance of Taking Vacation Time.* July 5. Accessed October 25, 2018. https://osg.ca/importance-of-taking-vacation-time/.

Holy Bible. n.d. "Holy Bible." In *The Holy Bible containing the Old and New Testaments*, 937. Camden, New Jersey 08103: Thomas Nelson Inc.

n.d. *Human Origins.* http://humanorigins.si.edu/evidence/human-fossils/species/homo-sapiens.

Johnson, Fodor's Travel: Holly. 2018. *10 Best Caribbean Islands for Family Travel.* November 30. Accessed December 22, 2020. https://www.fodors.com/world/caribbean/experiences/news/10-best-caribbean-islands-for-family-travel.

Kemmis, Sam. 2021. *How Much Are Your Airline Miles and Hotel Points Worth in 2021?* February 18. Accessed February 21, 2021. https://www.nerdwallet.com/article/travel/airline-miles-and-hotel-points-valuations.

koa. 2021. *KOA.* Accessed March 27, 2021. https://koa.com/.

Mattison, Linsay D. 2019. *The Best Family Reunion Spot in Every State.* April 22. Accessed March 27, 2021. https://www.tasteofhome.com/collection/the-best-family-reunion-spot-in-every-state/.

National Human genome Research Institute. 2018. *Genetics vs. Genomics Fact Sheet.* September 7. Accessed January 5, 2021. https://www.genome.gov/about-genomics/fact-sheets/Genetics-vs-Genomics#:~:text=All%20human%20beings%20are%2099.9,about%20the%20causes%20of%20diseases.

National Park Service. 2020. *Find a Campground.* March 23. Accessed March 27, 2021. https://www.nps.gov/subjects/camping/campground.htm.

Bibliography

Network, United Nations Population Information. n.d. *The Family, its roles, Composition and Structure.* http://www.un.org/popin/icpd/prepcomm/official/rap/RAP4.html.

Pennington, Emily. 2020. *The Best Place to Camp in Every State.* August 12. Accessed March 27, 2021. https://www.cntraveler.com/gallery/the-best-place-to-camp-in-every-state.

Plowright, tripsavvy: Teresa. 2019. *5 Destinations for Family Vacations in Mexico.* September 29. Accessed December 22, 2020. https://www.tripsavvy.com/mexico-vacations-for-families-3267056.

Project Management Institute. 2017. *A Guide To The Project Management Body Of Knowledge: PMBOK GUIDE.* Newtown Square: Project Management Institute.

Reeve, David. 2020. *15 Best Family Reunion Resorts, Places, & Venues – Everyone Will Love!* August 11. Accessed March 27, 2021. https://familydestinationsguide.com/best-family-reunion-resorts/.

Romano, Andrea. 2020. *24 of the Most Scenic Places to Camp in the United States.* June 18. Accessed March 27, 2021. https://www.travelandleisure.com/trip-ideas/nature-travel/most-scenic-campgrounds-in-us.

Seaney, Rick. 2019. *Cheapest Days to Fly and Best Time to Buy Airline Tickets.* December 23. Accessed February 21, 2021. https://www.farecompare.com/travel-advice/tips-from-air-travel-insiders/.

Shaffer, Leah. 2016. *How Sleep Can Heal Our Brains.* February 24. Accessed October 25, 2018. https://www.pbs.org/wgbh/nova/article/healing-sleep/.

Stapen, Candyce H. 2019. *12 Best Resorts for Family Reunions.* December 2. Accessed March 27, 2021. https://www.familyvacationcritic.com/10-best-resorts-for-family-reunions/art/.

Sula Hood, PHD, MPH. n.d. *AFRICAN AMERICAN FAMILY REUNION PARTNERSHIPS AS A CULTURALLY APPROPRIATE APPROACH FOR ADDRESSING HEALTH DISPARITIES.* Indianapolis: Indiana University Purde University.

Trainor, Meghan. 2014. *All About That Bass.* Comp. Meghan Trainor and Kevin Kadish.

Travel, U.S. News. n.d. *Best Family Beach Vacations in the U.S.* Accessed December 22, 2020. https://travel.usnews.com/rankings/best-family-beach-vacations-in-the-usa/.

Wikipedia. n.d. *List of minimum annual leave by country.* Accessed October 25, 2018. https://en.wikipedia.org/wiki/List_of_minimum_annual_leave_by_country.

—. n.d. *Who Dat?* https://en.wikipedia.org/wiki/Who_Dat%3F.

Wikipedia, The Free Encyclopedia. 2020. *Family Reunion.* June 26. Accessed January 17, 2021. https://en.wikipedia.org/wiki/Family_reunion.

Wikipedia, the free encyclopedia. 2021. *Hatfield-McCoy Feud.* January 3. Accessed January 16, 2021. https://en.wikipedia.org/wiki/Hatfield%E2%80%93McCoy_feud.

—. n.d. *Murphy"s Law.* Accessed April 3, 2021. https://en.wikipedia.org/wiki/Murphy%27s_law.

Wofford, Karyn. 2019. *9 Best Budget Resorts for Family Reunions.* September 25. Accessed March 27, 2021. https://www.tripstodiscover.com/best-budget-resorts-for-family-reunions/.

Yogerst, Joe. 2020. *25 Best Lake Vacations in the U.S.* July 14. Accessed February 14, 2021. https://www.travelandleisure.com/trip-ideas/summer-vacations/americas-best-lake-vacations#.

ABOUT THE AUTHOR

Henry Lee Thomas is a "Renaissance man" whose skills and interests span many areas. He was born in Georgia, a middle child from a large family.

By profession he is a project engineer and pricing analyst with a broad interest in many subjects. He has a non-ending thirst for knowledge. His work career has taken him from California to Pennsylvania to Virginia, while his personal life has taken him all over the United States as well as Mexico, Europe, and the Caribbean.

He is also a poet, musician, photographer, and observer of life. This diverse background, along with his introspective way of thinking, allows him to see poetry from a unique perspective.

His other publications include *Mental Streams: Poems of the Heart and Soul* (2020), *Poems in the Keys of Life* (2019), and *Men's Guide to Being a Single Parent* (2014).

His work has also appeared in the Spillwords Press (November 2020) and the Nzuri Journal of Coastline College (May 2021).

He writes about anything that he finds interesting and of which he feels he has something to say.

He has a Bachelor of Arts in Mathematics from Oberlin College and a Master of Operations Research from the University of Iowa.

The Family Reunion Bible

INDEX

A

accommodations, 12, 28, 42, 43, 44, 46, 49, 58, 59, 60, 62, 74
activities, 8, 12, 14, 15, 16, 18, 26, 29, 31, 32, 37, 40, 47, 48, 61, 62, 67, 68, 73, 74, 79, 80, 85, 86, 88, 93, 94, 97, 98
Africa, xi, 1
all-inclusive, 67, 68, 69, 72
ancestors, 11, 77, 78, 79
attractions, 44, 64, 75
Auctions, 33
audience, 84
Awards, 36, 87

B

Bake Sales, 33
banners, 30
Banquet, 59, 88
Beach, xi, 44, 45, 59
beverages, 67
Bible, xi, 1, 2, 3, 7
Birth, 77
birthdays, 14
blog, 23
budget, 2, 10, 11, 13, 15, 17, 28, 29, 30, 31, 44, 48, 49, 68, 74
Budget, 28, 62, 105
buffet, 69

C

cameras, 34
campgrounds, 41, 60
Cemetery, 77
certificates, 36, 87
charts, 98
Checklist, 39, 121, 123
children, 1, 12, 36, 38, 53, 67, 82, 88
Church, 77
Code of Conduct, 38, 115, 117
communication methods, 20, 25
conference room, 15, 30, 39, 40, 74, 87
Contests, 97
cooperative cooking, 69, 70
Covid-19, 3, 50
COVID-19, 3, 4, 50, 91
cruise ships, 49, 50

D

decorations, 14, 15, 30, 94
DNA, 7, 77, 79, 157
Donations, 34
DoorDash, 72

E

email address, 14, 20
Emancipation, 7
entertainment, 48, 69
Escape Room, 77
ethnic, 7, 79

F

Facebook, 318
family history, 11, 77, 78, 79
Family Poem, iv
family reunion, xi, 2, 3, 4, 7, 8, 10, 11, 12, 13, 14, 15, 18, 21, 23, 25, 26, 27, 28, 29, 32, 33, 34, 36, 37, 39, 42, 43, 44, 45, 47, 51, 52, 59, 62, 64, 66, 69, 70, 73, 75, 76, 79, 80, 84, 86, 87, 88, 90, 92, 93, 94, 97, 98
Family reunion Month, 7
family website, 23, 27, 34
FAQ, 27
fishing license, 31
Fundraising, 13

G

games, 22, 31, 69, 74, 79, 80, 81, 97
genealogy, 7, 14, 78, 79
gift baskets, 16
God, iii, 1, 2, 11
Google Map, 41
Grubhub, 72
Guest book, 40

The Family Reunion Bible

H

handouts, 16, 18, 75, 83
Hatfield and McCoy, 37
History, 5, 7, 46, 77
hotel, 41, 62, 64
hotels, 46, 62, 67

I

ideas, 4, 34, 94
income, 28, 33
insurance, 91, 92
Internet, 41, 59, 67
Invitations, 29, 31

K

kickoff meetings, 26, 27

L

labels, 85
Laptop, 82
Locations, xi, 49, 95, 99, 133
lodging, 11, 12, 14, 15, 16, 28, 30, 31, 36, 37, 38, 39, 43, 48, 58, 59, 62, 67, 93, 117

M

Maps, 16, 41
medical, 92
meetings, 14, 25, 80
Mementos, 30
Memories, 18
menus, 70
Mexican Fiesta, 30
Microsoft Excel, 22, 29, 97
Microsoft Publisher, 21
Microsoft Word, 21
mission statement, 11
money, 2, 17, 28, 33, 34, 59, 68, 69, 70, 93
multi-generational American family, 1
Music, 46, 75

N

Name tags, 17, 40
National Park, 47, 60
national parks, 44
newsletters, 15, 21

O

Oberlin College, xi, 313

P

payments, 14, 16, 27, 28
photographer, 18, 31, 85, 313
picnic, 31, 84, 86
Picnic, 61
planner, xi, 48
planning, xi, 2, 3, 4, 7, 8, 9, 10, 11, 12, 13, 14, 15, 17, 20, 21, 22, 25, 26, 27, 28, 29, 32, 39, 40, 43, 44, 58, 67, 68, 75, 81, 82, 88, 90, 91, 93, 94, 117, 118
planning team, 10, 12, 14, 22, 26, 27, 28, 29, 39, 40, 117, 118
postage, 21
Potluck, 69
presentations, 29, 83
printing, 77
prizes, 31, 87
project management, 10
puzzles, 77

R

Raffles, 34
recipes, 33, 70, 76, 85
refreshments, 74
registration, 39, 40
rentals, 29, 30, 62
reservations, 29, 68, 92
resort, 24, 41, 62, 63, 64, 65, 68, 72, 97
resorts, 46, 62, 65, 67, 69
reunions, iii, xi, 1, 2, 4, 7, 8, 10, 11, 12, 14, 15, 23, 26, 32, 34, 35, 39, 43, 44, 46, 47, 51, 52, 62, 66, 74, 77, 80, 81, 83, 90, 92, 94
Ritz Carlton, 58
rules of engagement, 38
RV sites, 60

S

Scenic Places, 60
scrapbooks, 78, 84
signs, 34
Social media, 25
software, 14, 21, 24, 97
souvenirs, 30
state park, 31
strawman, 94

surveys, 21, 22, 26, 48, 81

T

talent show, 86, 87
team building, 80
theme, 13, 14, 15, 16, 17, 21, 26, 30, 34, 75, 84, 94
ticket, 53
Timothy 5:8
    Bible passage, 1
Tours, 32, 87
train routes, 53
transportation, 11, 28, 32, 43, 44, 51, 52, 54, 67, 69, 87, 88
T-shirts, 15
Twitter, 318

U

Uber Eats, 72
United Nations, 1

V

Venues, 62
video, 18, 25, 74
videographer, 18, 31

W

websites, 16, 22, 78
Wise Men, 42

Z

Zoom, 25

What Did You Think About The Family Reunion Bible?

First of all, thank you for purchasing this book. I know you could have picked a number of other books on planning family reunions, but you picked this book and for that, I am extremely grateful.

I hope that it was very beneficial to you in planning your own reunion. If so, it would be really nice if you could share this book with your friends and family by posting to Facebook and/or Twitter.

Also, I would appreciate it if you could take some time to post a review on Amazon, Barnes & Noble, or any other place of purchase. Your feedback and support will help this author to greatly improve his writing craft and make his future books even better.

Thank you!

www.ingramcontent.com/pod-product-compliance
Lightning Source LLC
Chambersburg PA
CBHW081305070526
44578CB00006B/807